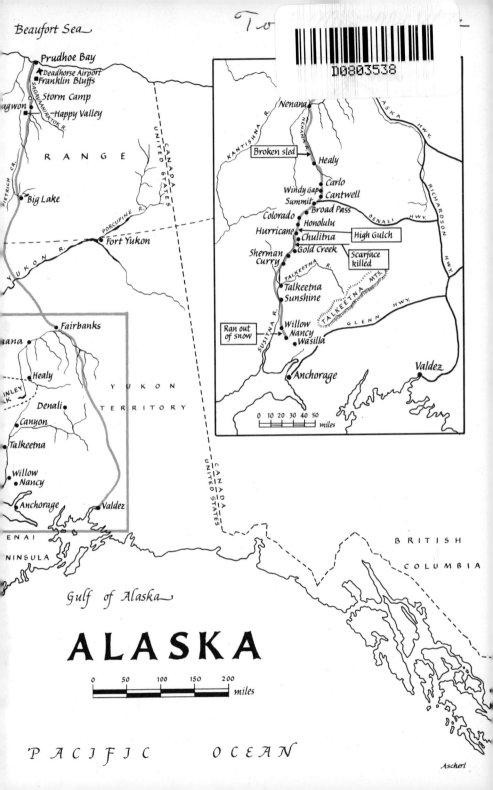

Beaufort Sea

Prudhoe Bay
Deadhorse Airport
Franklin Bluffs
Storm Camp
Happy Valley
agwon

R A N G E

Big Lake

Fort Yukon

Fairbanks

Healy

Denali

Canyon

Talkeetna

Willow
Nancy

Anchorage

Valdez

Y U K O N

T E R R I T O R Y

CANADA
UNITED STATES

ENAI

NINSULA

Gulf of Alaska

ALASKA

0   50   100   150   200
miles

P A C I F I C   O C E A N

Nenana

Broken sled → Healy

Carlo
Windy Gap   Cantwell
Summit
Colorado   Broad Pass
Honolulu
Hurricane   Chulitna   High Gulch
Sherman   Gold Creek
Curry   Scarface
killed

Talkeetna
Sunshine

Ran out   Willow
of snow   Nancy
Wasilla

Anchorage

Valdez

TALKEETNA MTS.

GLENN   HWY.

0 10 20 30 40 50
miles

BRITISH

COLUMBIA

D0803538

Ascherl

DOGSLED

A true tale of the North

Slim Randles

WINCHESTER PRESS

Library of Congress Cataloging in Publication Data

Randles, Slim.
    Dogsled: a true tale of the North.

    SUMMARY: A reporter recounts adventures of his
adopted life in Alaska and particularly his grueling
dog team expeditions.
        1. Alaska—Description and travel—1959.
2. Randles, Slim. 3. Dogsledding—Alaska—Personal
narratives. [1. Alaska—Description and travel.
2. Randles, Slim. 3. Dogsledding—Alaska—Personal
narratives]. I. Title.
F910.R36   917.98'04'50924   76-22211
ISBN 0-87691-186-6

WINCHESTER is a Trademark of Olin Corporation used by
Winchester Press, Inc. under authority and control of
the Trademark Proprietor.

    Book and jacket design by Joseph P. Ascherl

    Published by Winchester Press
    205 East 42nd Street, New York 10017

    Printed in the United States of America

To the memory of
LAWRENCE S. FANNING

DOGSLED

A true tale of the North

1

Some things are sacred to a youngster, and in my boyhood it was the weekly drama of *Sergeant Preston of the Yukon* and his beloved dog, King. Visiting relatives, curfew, or the danger of my father's ever-handy belt . . . nothing could keep this avid listener from his appointed post near the radio.

Sometimes wrapped in bedsheets to symbolize a snow-covered parka, I would crouch in the humid air of southern California to listen as my hero whisked his dog team hundreds of miles through the frozen North to bring about Truth, Justice, and the Canadian Way.

In stentorian tones, Preston would say, "Pierre Le Noir . . . eh, Inspector? Murdered five Cree Indians? Stole from twenty trappers? Jumped the claims of forty men, eh? Well, we can't have that! His hideout is only one hundred miles from here over two mountain ranges, Inspector.   Should be a little late for dinner tonight, but we'll bring him in . . . eh, King?"

"Woof!"

"Good boy.   Good fella.   Now to the team and away!   On King!   On you huskies!"

At the crack of the whip, the yelping dogs would leap into their harness and surge through driving snowstorms over two mountain ranges, where King would jump Le Noir (maiming him for life), and have the Sergeant back to report with his man in less than half an hour.

Twenty years later, however, King must have died, and the quality of sled dogs in general degenerated beyond belief, for I found myself dressed in a real parka, in a real snowdrift, with a real team of eight dogs, and things weren't going so well.

The whole team was floundering in six feet of soft powder snow in the middle of the majestic Alaska Range, and I was close to collapse.   Waves of exhaustion rippled over me as I struggled to help the dogs gain a few feet toward the railroad tracks, the only broken "trail" in this part of Alaska.

My body wasn't ready for the strain of being on trail, however.   Months of desk work on the staff of a newspaper had made it soft, and the warm temperatures and heavy clothing made breathing very difficult.   My left arm hung limp and useless by my

2

side, due to a heavy pain in my chest.   At 27, I was much too young for a heart attack, but I could think of no other explanation.

Again the snow gave way, plunging me into a body-shaped pit, and the heavy sled crashed down over my chest.   I could no longer fight it.

As the darkness of the faint ran through me, I thought of my long "study" of Sergeant Preston, and wondered how I came from the security of office life in California to be gasping beneath the steel-edged runners of a dog sled in February of 1970 in Alaska.

Then blackness forced my body to rest.

2

My first trip to Alaska, which lasted several months, occurred in 1966 while on assignment for some California newspapers. The first rush of awe for the scenery soon gave way to a deep appreciation for the people who live here. However, not until a certain summer night that year, on a homestead some eighty miles from Anchorage, did the determination to become an Alaskan myself first begin to settle.

Given the name of a friend's relative on this homestead, I hitchhiked out to the dense spruce and birch forest near the town of Wasilla, and was invited to spend a few days at the home of Gene Schilber. Schilber's cabin was a large, two-storey place set on the edge of his required forty acres of cleared field.

Schilber had "had it made" in California. He

4

had, at various times, been head of an advertising agency, a professional cartoonist, and a noted athlete.

"Had it made?" he asked. "That's a matter of how you look at it, I guess. I went to work . . . came home . . . opened a beer . . . watched television . . . and worried about paying all the bills. Now just look . . ."

His arm made a wide sweep around the rustic room.

As each item of furniture was pointed out with pride, crude though it be, I was quickly told that it was all paid for.

Gene's eyes flashed as he extolled the virtues of bush living in Alaska, nearly letting the moose steaks burn. It seemed as though the chamber of commerce had caught up with me four miles from a paved road. As the monologue drew on into the wee hours, however, I gathered that much of Schilber's romance with homesteading was in the absence of bills.

"You, my friend, are absolutely right!" he said, pounding on the hewn birch table.

"Why, in the States, you spend all your waking time worrying about bills . . . yes, and even dreaming about them at night!"

He continued.

"Those poor slobs down there keep plugging away

for fifty years, and what do they have? MORE BILLS! Yes, by God! Up here we may not have enough money some of the time, but who needs it? Not US! Those guys spend twenty years of their lives buying a house that only lasts ten. They have building inspectors, termite inspectors, tax inspectors, and inspector's inspectors. They have a tax on everything they touch or buy. They have to buy licenses for the car, the house, the wife, the kids, even the stupid family dog! Is that any way to live? OF COURSE NOT! Now you take Alaska . . ."

"You mean to say you don't have taxes and licenses up here?"

His face took on a glow as he wiped some of the froth from his mouth.

"Of course we have—only . . ." he leaned close so that the neighbors, a full mile down the road, couldn't overhear, "we have so much room in this blasted bush country, that they have a hell of a time even FINDING you, let alone taxing you!"

"Why," he went on, "I once heard of a guy living out on the Chain (The Aleutian Islands) so far back in the bush that half his army hitch was up before he got his draft notice. Now THAT, by George, is living in the bush!"

"But Gene," I said, "what do you do for a living?" You still have to buy grub, even if there isn't any rent to pay."

"Well," he said, sheepishly, "you see, I'm disabled—get my checks for that—isn't much, but keeps me going. Then, too, we live off the land quite a bit."

"Disabled? But you were telling me about playing pro ball, and boxing, and you look great."

"Purely a superficial impression," he said, waving away my question. "I might look like I'm in good shape, but inside I'm a mess. Can't hardly take a step without pain shooting through every inch of my body. Been that way ever since the accident."

Gene looked over his shoulder, waiting.

"Accident?"

Like a flash, he resumed his pacing and cleared his throat.

"It was awful. Just terrible. Nearly died, you know. Didn't my aunt tell you? No, of course not. She didn't know. Kept the awful truth from the family."

"What happened?"

"Froze my lungs. Nearly died, you know. Just terrible, but it had to be done."

"What had to be done?"

"Why, the men had to be saved, of course, and no one else would do it. Did you expect I wouldn't do anything? Did you think I could stand idly by and let my fellow man die unaided at the top of a two-hundred-foot tower in a driving blizzard just because I might lose my insignificant life in the attempt? No, by God!"

"You see," he continued, "it was at one of those DEW line stations, in the frozen Arctic wasteland, and it was January of the coldest year we've had up here.

"Yes, it was seventy below, with a fifty-mile-an-hour wind, even though the sun was shining . . ."

"In January? But I thought . . ."

"Of course—the sun wasn't shining too brightly. In fact, in January, by God, all you can see of it is a glow toward the south, and THAT makes it pretty damn cold! Yes . . . as I was saying, it was so cold that the machinery operating the bucket lift to the top of the tower froze solid, leaving two men stranded at the top. It often gets that cold in the frozen windswept Arctic wastelands, you know. That old tundra turns into permafrost that solids the ground up so hard, nothing can penetrate it. Why I recall one time up north that . . ."

"What about the men on the tower?"

"I was getting to them. Yes, by God, there they were, clinging to the frozen steel girders as if to life itself. The wind was unmercifully whipping by their frightened faces on that windswept pinnacle of

8

loneliness. Yes, by George, there they were—with no chance at all of coming down. All alone up there in the cold. Those of us on the ground knew we were looking at two dead men."

His voice became soft.

"Have you ever seen two live men that you knew were going to be dead in a few minutes? Well, I have, and there they were, clinging like leeches to the girders of that hurricane-hit promontory.

"Some of the boys on the ground were frantically trying to thaw the machinery to let the boys ride down in the buckets, but we all knew that it was futile. The men were dead—just as dead as if they had been lying in their caskets. Several of the boys were saying prayers for the men. But not me! No, by God, I was busy trying to figure how to save them from their certain death. That's the Alaskan Way, you know.

"Then, all of a sudden, it came to me. Of course! Why hadn't I thought of it before? It was the only way!"

He gave me another of those sly looks.

"What could you do for them, Gene?"

"Why, the only thing possible. There was a cable going up from the engine to the top of the tower where the men were. I made up my mind, and before anyone could stop me, I went up the cable hand-over-hand."

9

His voice lowered to a penetrating softness.

"It was a trial, I can tell you. There I was, going slowly hand-over-hand up that frozen cable, each new grip bringing sharp biting pain into every muscle and joint. I thought I was never going to reach the top. The icy wind whipped across my frozen face. More than once I was tempted to go back—but no. I couldn't. Not with those two men stranded at the top, their only hope for survival resting in me as I swung slowly toward them up the cable.

"The wind shrieked louder and louder as I drew nearer the top. The blizzard howled around me, coating my body with snow until I was a white-coated figure swaying perilously close to death in the wind.

"At last I reached the top. The men were so glad to see me, they nearly hugged me, but didn't, of course, as they would have been blown to oblivion in a second.

"One of the men, the braver of the two, decided he would descend the swaying cable in the manner I had come up. He knew now that it was humanly possible. I helped him get a grip, and then sent him off down the cable.

"I waited until he was about halfway down, and then turned to the other man to help him start down. But the other man, who was called Tiny, and weighed three hundred pounds, was afraid to go. I tried to tell him through the screaming gale that he could make it, but he wouldn't listen. There was only one possible thing I could do to save his life."

"What was that?"

"I had to knock him out and carry him down to safety. On the way down, I could feel my lungs freezing. The frost grabs them quick, you know. By the time I reached the bottom, I was a ruined man. I hovered between life and death on a delicate thread for several weeks, but I had saved the lives of two of my fellow men, and I felt it was a small enough price to pay.

"They were going to put stories about me in the papers, and even talked of giving me some kind of medal, but my modesty wouldn't allow it. It wasn't the Alaskan Way of doing things."

I agreed, wondering silently just how magnificently his lungs must've worked before being frozen.

3

In the fall of 1969, I again crossed the border to my new home, nearly broke, and very cold. Heading at once for Schilber's homestead, I learned from neighbors that he had gone to live in Anchorage. Finding him wasn't too hard, and we talked over old times with the help of a few beers.

Anchorage is a bad place to roam without money. My remaining twenty dollars didn't last long, and I soon found myself pounding the pavement looking for work.

Through all this time, Schilber had taken me in as a roommate (nonpaying), and had bought me warm clothes and meals until I could get on my feet. He was staying in a motel on the edge of town, and had to sneak me in the back door, as the manager wasn't supposed to know I was there. Later, the manager found out, but conveniently and kindly looked the other way. My bed was the floor, but it was much more comfortable than the sub-zero temperatures Anchorage was experiencing at that time.

While all the sneaking in the back door and looking for work went on, Gene bought me several books on self-confidence. One in particular caught my imagination, and I soon structured a master plan to earn a fortune through belief in myself.

The first part of the plan I followed immediately. I wrote a note to myself, taping it to the mirror. It read, "This year, I *will* earn $50,000!"

Ignoring the nasty remarks the maids passed as they cleaned the room, I would look at the paper and repeat in a deep voice full of conviction, "This year I will *earn* $50,000!"

Then, even more confident, I would exclaim, "This year, I WILL earn $50,000!"

And I did, too. Almost. That is, I felt that I earned that much. I just took home a little less, and only missed by a paltry $45,000.

My original scheme of founding a magazine fell through when I wrote to my "backer" in California, and didn't receive so much as a Christmas card. That left me with little choice.

Anchorage has two large daily newspapers and, as luck would have it, I landed jobs on both papers the same day.

There are two basic types of journalism. The first, and by far the more prevalent, is the "wait-for-it-to-happen-and-then-quote-somebody" kind. This type dates back to the pre-TV days when papers still got "scoops" on the news, and reporters could run in waving papers and yelling "Stop the press!"

The other style, personal journalism or "in-depth" reporting, is actually much older. It hasn't been around much since the New York *Herald* sent Stanley to Africa in search of Dr. Livingstone I presume, but it is coming back.

The Anchorage *Daily Times*, the state's largest paper, is an excellent example of the first type of reporting.

The Anchorage *Daily News*, publishing each morning, is Alaska's closest tie with the new personal journalism. Smaller by half than the *Times*, and financially troubled since its beginnings in 1946 as "the other paper," the *Daily News* has had an uphill climb simply to exist.

If a problem arises in some village, the *Times* reporter calls a state official and asks about it. The *News* reporter calls the official, then gets on a plane, and spends a week in the village, scooping up not only the problem itself, but the underlying feelings of the community, the history of the problem, and the "feel" of the place.

I chose the *Daily News*. I was more suited to that kind of journalism. Also, they offered me twenty dollars a week more than the *Times* did.

The following day, I dropped in at the *Times* to let them know I had chosen the smaller paper. *Times* Managing Editor, Bill Tobin, (the man who made a tour of the United States trying to find a town without hippies in it), told me at that meeting I would regret my decision.

"Not only won't they (the *Daily News*) pay you anything," he had said, "but you won't get the opportunity to cover the stories you want."

One year and over 20,000 miles later, the memory of that talk keeps me warm on cold winter nights.

4

My first job with the *Daily News* was "on the desk"—a combination of editor and reporter. At this job, a man writes headlines, edits some copy, and takes some stories over the phone and writes them.

Then, too, he drinks coffee a lot.

It isn't as grandiose as the managing editor's job (he gets to have his name printed on the editorial page each day, with his title), but is more fun than covering weddings or wrestling matches.

Still, the job was an inside job, and I had always been an outside-type feature writer. Little by little, I began to ask my bosses Larry and Kay Fanning for assignments outside the office, and, when possible, they let me do them.

One of these opportunities came one day when the publicity chairman (unofficial) of the local dog mushers' club paid us a visit with some race results.

In no time at all, I had him cornered and was pumping questions about dog mushing at him so fast, that he finally gave in and agreed to give me a "mushing lesson" with some of his dogs that weekend.

The musher, Lloyd Haessler, was not a big name in racing. In fact, he hardly ever won anything at the races. He had a way of training lead dogs, though, that took one of his dogs, Chinook, to the world championship three years. Mostly, however, Lloyd ran his dogs for fun—and fun it was.

We drove to some snow-covered trails on Elmendorf Air Force Base one day, and after a lot of confusing harnessing of dogs, I climbed on the runners of a sled, pulled free the rope that held the team to the truck, and shot down a trail. The dogs ran smoothly and fast (they are silent when they run—King please take note) and I was able to keep up a conversation with Lloyd, who followed with a second team.

In the few miles we ran that day, my mind had become firm on one thing: I *would* become a dog musher.

On several other outings with Lloyd and his dogs, and through his patience, I learned the proper way to harness the dogs, and to snap on the two lengths of nylon rope that project from the main "tow line" running between the dogs. The short neckline

17

keeps the dog (in theory) facing the right way, and the longer tugline was fastened to the harness for him to pull.

Back at the office, I did a lot of serious thinking. The reason I had come north was to enjoy the country, and yet here I was working a regular shift indoors. What I had hoped for was adventure, but outside of weekend dog mushing excursions around the air force base, I had been getting precious little.

Could I combine adventure with reporting and still help the *Daily News?*

Chewing the problem over for several weeks, I hatched a plan: I would borrow a dog team and mush them from Fairbanks to Anchorage, writing stories about the adventure and the people I met along the way.

It took me three weeks to wipe the expression of terror off the Fannings' faces, but they finally agreed to let me try it. By this time, I had borrowed a team of dogs from a local musher, a sled from Tim Redington, and some equipment from various parties.

Then the musher who offered me the dogs backed out.

Driving by the dog pound that afternoon, I stopped in for a visit. To my surprise, there were a number of huskies, mixed husky-type dogs, and some other large dogs that had been impounded and were up for adoption.

After some talking, the S.P.C.A. agreed to let me have some dogs for the trip in return for some favorable publicity. I had always wanted to do something for dogs in a pound, anyway.

Tim Redington and I took a sled and one of his lead dogs to the pound and "auditioned" a number of them. Some refused to pull. Some pulled rather well—at first. Most of them at least looked in the right direction when the sled was going down the trail.

Choosing eight of the likeliest prospects, I left three others with Tim in reserve, should I need them later during the trip.

With these dogs (mostly strays named as we took their pictures), I was ready to leave the next day.

Then we had a conference.

The boss decided it would take too long to run from Fairbanks to Anchorage, so we decided I would leave McKinley Park headquarters and start south—about three hundred miles.

The following morning, eight dogs were loaded into a boxcar, the sled and gear into a freight car, and a scared musher into a passenger car.

As I rode along through the forest of the taiga (spruce and birch) belt of the Matanuska Valley, and later the treeless areas of the Alaska Range, I thought about what I had promised to do.

In my lap a newspaper proclaimed "Our Musher Will Save The Dogs." In my mind was the rumor I had heard that the dog mushers were giving odds of three-to-one against me making it.

In my zeal to have some fun and get out of the office, I had opened my mouth and maybe had gotten myself a peck of trouble.

As the train rocked slowly back and forth on the tracks, I bought many cups of coffee and mentally took stock of my "dog team."

Behind me several cars, snapped to a long picket chain, were:

Big Red—An ugly red dog, about ninety pounds, who had been a sled dog at one time. He enjoyed pulling.

Randolph—A Norwegian elkhound, the smallest of the bunch, who tried hard and had a good sense of humor.

Nameless—A Mackenzie husky who picked fights, chewed harness, and who was the subject of a naming contest for school children.

Big John—A huge Malemute pup (we later learned he was only eight months old) who wanted to learn, but was a coward at heart.

Shep—A German shepherd, about one year old,

20

who was friendly and eager to please.

Scarface—A white Samoyed with scars on his face (naturally) who was eager to get out of the pound, even if it meant pulling a sled to do it.

Jeff—A brown hound who showed no promise at all, got cold feet, wouldn't pull his share, and goofed off. He was taken along so that the musher wouldn't feel inferior to *all* the dogs.

Taffy—Our only girl dog (that's a polite way of saying she was a spayed bitch), she was pure white, pretty, demure, polite, and had a personality not unlike Penelope Pitstop. Unfortunately, if she did any work later, it was kept a big secret from the musher.

Not only were these dogs counting on me to find them homes through the publicity the trip would bring (they had all been sentenced to suffocate in the pressure tank the day before we left) but I was also responsible to the paper for their trust in me, and thousands of readers were counting on good copy.

My roommate was counting on my coming back alive, too. I still owed him a month's rent.

The Alaska Railroad cuts away from the roads at Talkeetna and winds on its twin steel trail through magnificent mountain country at a snail's pace. The slow pace enabled me to "case the joint" on the way up.

21

Only one place, Hurricane Gulch, had me worried. The bridge over the Gulch stretches four hundred yards over a chasm two-hundred ninety-six feet deep. It would be necessary to take the team over this trestle, as there is no going around it.

Under normal winter conditions, a musher could run down the frozen rivers. In February of 1970, however, Alaska was experiencing one of the mildest winters it had had in many years. Every river had open water and dangerous ice on it. It began to look more and more as though I would have to stick to the tracks themselves for the entire trip.

It was a strange winter. Up high in the mountains, near Broad Pass (which was not named for a woman), I would encounter snow far over my head, while in the Matanuska Valley little green things were beginning to poke up through the already-bare ground.

I stepped off the train at McKinley Park into a minus-four degree windstorm and began to unravel the chain that the dogs, in their excitement, had turned into steel spaghetti. With help, they were picketed. I located a wooden bench to sleep on in the station house, and collapsed for a few minutes to do some serious thinking.

"Randles," I said, "you scribbler of the priceless prose, you savior of impounded pooches—my boy, this time you really screwed up."

5

Blue Denham was the caretaker of the McKinley Park Hotel. It was easy to locate his rooms, as he and Mrs. Denham had the only lighted windows in the monstrous dark hotel. It was about one-hundred yards up the hill from the now-empty station-house-postoffice.

It was cold, and flakes of snow curled around the sparse trees in the yard. I was grateful for the warmth of the fire and the coffee.

After phoning my story in to the paper, I was invited to stay for dinner. Another guest that evening was Gordon Haber, the noted "wolf man" of McKinley Park. In his late twenties, Haber had lived with the wolves for two years at that time, and planned to spend another two before pulling out.

"Gordie" didn't actually live with the wolves, but stayed in a small cabin, 22 miles back in, near the wolves' den. He spent most of his time photographing them, watching them, and taking notes for a book.

Haber wanted to save the wolves.

Saving wolves, in my opinion, is a most admirable profession. The McKinley Park wolf, I soon learned, might be protected by the laws of the national park system, but not necessarily by man himself. According to Haber, dozens of wolves are taken out of the park each year by poachers who shoot the wolves from planes, then land nearby, load the carcasses, and take off before they are detected.

Haber claimed to know of a dozen men from Fairbanks who do this constantly, and nearly three times that many from Anchorage. (The federal Fish and Wildlife people later told me they were aware of the poaching, but seriously doubted Haber's figures.)

The wolf bounty ($50) was meant to provide an additional source of income to Native peoples in the far-flung bush areas. In theory, at least, this would mean that only a handful of wolves would be taken from each village, as dog team was the only transportation for most villagers at that time. Rarely would a musher with a team of large dogs come in sight of the timid wolf.

What usually happens, however, happened.

It wasn't long until hunters in Cessna 180's and Super Cubs were zooming around the skies with shotguns loaded with double-ought buck.

24

Some wolves died instantly, but many more Alaskan wolves today pack around some man-made ballast as they try to run down rabbits, squirrels, and sick caribou.

Haber carried on about the subject for several hours, and I finally asked him why he chose to live with wolves. After hearing the altruistic motives, I learned that Haber was actually looking for more initials. It seems that he had worked in school very hard for six years, which entitled him to put four initials behind his name. These four years, he explained, were so he could put three more on the end of the four he'd already accumulated.

When I learned that it had taken him four years to be able to put the initials "B.S." after his name, I mentioned that he hadn't been very efficient. He seemed puzzled, so I explained that I had been in the newspaper business not three months before many readers would have willingly given me those particular initials *gratis*.

He didn't seem too impressed.

Whatever else can be said about Haber, he plays good guitar and enjoys singing. In this country, that is an accomplishment.

Haber and Blue Denham agreed to come down and help me "hook up" in the morning (one seldom gets free comedy acts at McKinley Park in winter) and I said goodnight.

A winter night at the park is lonely and cold.

A hard inch of icy snow crusted the ground in patches. Stunted trees, seldom exceeding fifteen feet in height, swayed in the wind. Moose tracks cut across the path in front of me, and the light from the station welcomed me to a warm place to bunk.

What lay ahead?

In the morning I was to harness eight green dogs to a clumsy, overloaded, antique racing sled, with almost no snow to run on, and start back for Anchorage.

Rolling out the sleeping bag on the bench, I watched the wind-driven flakes outside against the porch light. They made a filigree pattern, dancing a lacy ballet in a black night. Whatever waited out there was hidden now by darkness and by snow. By morning, I'd have to face it.

I smoked one more pipe and watched the swirl. Perhaps they would put a sufficient coating of snow on the ground for the sled. I'd find out in the morning.

The dogs were all asleep in the lee of the shed. The gear was all double checked. My clothes were clean. I wrote a letter to my family in California.

Sleep was long in coming, and still the flakes danced.

6

In the still half-dark early winter morning I rolled my sleeping bag and picked up the dog food bucket, lashing them to the sled.

I laid out the rigging for the dogs and turned to greet Blue. His wife, he said, had breakfast ready, and asked if I'd join them. I have yet to refuse a free meal.

After breakfast, the Denhams, along with Haber and a friend, came down to see me off.

With their help, all eight dogs were harnessed and snapped to the tuglines. Up on the Bering Sea and other open areas, Eskimos quite often use a "fan hitch": each dog is attached to the sled by a separate line, and they fan out rather than walk directly behind another dog. In the woods, of course, this arrangement would be disastrous the minute the first tree came along.

Early prospectors used a single-file hitch, with tug lines running on each side of each dog, similar to the way horses are attached to wagons. This is especially handy in new, unbroken snow, where the musher has to walk ahead of the dogs, packing the snow with his snowshoes.

The tandem hitch, or "Indian hitch", was developed for two reasons. For one, having the dogs coupled, that is, two-by-two, enables a musher to use the strength of many dogs and halve the distance from the sled to the lead dog. This is most desirable, especially when commands must be given in a high wind.

By the time the tandem hitch became popular, the Alaskan interior was a mesh of hard-packed, wide trails, and breaking trail took place only for half a day after a fresh snow.

Why half a day? The main trails of Alaska, the early day freeways, were well travelled. At the end of each day's mushing was a roadhouse, offering bunks and food and laughter. After a snow, the musher would pack trail for half a day until he met a musher coming the other way, packing trail as he came. From that point until the next roadhouse, both men ran on packed trail.

The country, in those early days, was far from being a trackless wilderness. The dog trails of yesteryear were much more extensive than the handfull of highways Alaska has today. The trails have

28

grown over and disappeared, replaced by a landing strip at each village. Many old-timers are quick to tell people that today Alaska is far more primitive and untrod than it was sixty years ago.

The tandem hitch is used almost exclusively now. It combines compactness and control, and is advocated by cross-country mushers and racers alike. A long central line extends from the "bridle" of the sled (just between and behind the brush bow and the runners) and the harness of the lead dog, or dogs. In my case, I used a double-lead—a one-foot length of nylon rope with a snap at each end to connect the collars of the lead dogs.

Behind the lead dogs, at intervals of about eight feet, the tuglines extend from the main towline. The dogs are snapped to these, one on each side of the towline. The number of pairs of dogs is optional. In my case, there were four pairs. Each pair has a position name, and each has a job to do that differs just slightly from the others.

Directly in front of the sled are the wheel dogs. These are usually the biggest, slowest and strongest. They must provide the heavy jerk that breaks the runners free of the ice each morning, and do most of the pulling when topping over a slight rise. This is also the usual place to put untrained dogs, as the musher is closer to them, and can untangle them.

Directly in front of the wheel dogs are the second

wheelers. These are also usually heavier and stronger than the others.

In front of the second-wheelers are the swing dogs. They are usually lighter, faster, and better-trained dogs that help the leaders make turns.

The lead dogs, of course, are the brains of the outfit (in a well-trained team). They are light, fast, and the best trained of the team.

Comparing lead dogs with the wheel dogs is like comparing the jobs of quarterback and defensive tackle on a football team. The first gets all the glory—the second does all the dirty work.

That, however, is a well-trained team. I was facing eight dogs that had never run before (except Red), and I had no idea where each dog would eventually end up.

The snow was blowing at thirty miles per hour, the temperature read minus four. It was cold.

The men helped me aim the lead dogs toward the dirt road leading to Cantwell. I stepped aboard the sled runners and hollered "Hike!"

To no one's particular surprise, the lead dogs turned and ran back to me for some petting.

Leading them out to the front, I pointed down the road and yelled "Hike!" a little louder. They thought it was a new game, and jumped on me.

Finally, I grabbed the connecting necklines of the lead dogs, and pulled them down the road. They

30

came, all right, but I had forgotten six other dogs behind them. Two of them started a fight. I broke it up with the butt end of my whip, went back to the lead dogs, and dragged them ahead. This time the sled moved, just a little.

After a few minutes, the lead dogs were content to walk beside me at "heel" while the sled moved. This continued for a blissful hundred yards. Then Big John, back in the wheel position, became frightened. He pulled half out of his harness, slipped his collar completely, and turned and jumped in the sled. His weight knocked the small sled over on its side.

Walking back, my nerves already short with the high wind and cold, I extricated John's furry bulk from the sled wreckage.

After relashing the load, and reharnessing John, I turned and got a glimpse of my four friends watching silently in the storm. They stood like parka-clad statues, and if they were laughing, they were at least polite about it.

Back to the leaders, grabbing the neckline and dragging them back to action again. This time, the sled came along more easily for another hundred yards.

Then I ran out of snow.

Gravel . . . stretching as far as the eye could see (which, in the storm, was about seventy-five feet). The week before I arrived at the Park, the area had experienced one of those mid-winter phenomena known locally as a Chinook. Mysteriously, the constant north wind shifted around to the south, raising the temperature to fifty above for three days. The snow that didn't melt was blown away. Only scattered patches in the shade remained of the winter's accumulation.

Hitting the gravel, the hundred-fifty-pound sled suddenly gained about six hundred pounds— according to the dogs. They balked, they quarreled. They lunged and were jerked back. The drag was worsened, I found, because the sled had been loaded incorrectly and was nose-heavy. The runners behind the sled waved in the air without the musher's weight to hold them down. The sled wobbled down the road like a drunken fishing lure.

I dragged the dogs until they walked well, then released them again and walked beside them. They took to it easier this time. Gradually I slowed my walking speed until more and more of the dogs passed me. In another hundred yards I was even with the sled. I quickly stepped on the runners to add the ballast and the sled ground to a halt.

The lead dogs came running back to me. Randolph did a pirouette, tangling himself and several teammates.

Grabbing the lead dogs, who were now attempting to crawl under the sled, I dragged them back to the front. Placing a foot directly on the rump of one of the lead dogs, I then reached behind me to untangle the mess.

Three dogs sat or lay in various positions, having miraculously thrown half-hitches over their legs, noses, and anything else they could locate. Here was a perfect granny knot: there a cunningly executed sheepshank.

At the bottom of this nylon-husky knot was Randolph, who had not only tied up two other dogs, but had succeeded in lashing himself securely to himself. He grinned at me sheepishly. This was my introduction to Randolph's mania with knots. Right then, I was ready to give him to the Navy, the Boy Scouts, or anyone else who liked rope demonstrations.

Now, I used to do a little calf roping in rodeos, and have untied many more calves than I ever actually caught. I was no greenhorn at hogtying, but this was beyond me.

After some struggle, I discovered that by unsnapping the dogs from both the tuglines and the necklines, I could make the job go faster. Doing so, I then learned that Red enjoyed chasing snowshoe rabbits.

Half an hour later, Red was back in harness,

thoroughly chastised, and Randolph was again securely fastened by a series of bowlines and barrel hitches to the two dogs behind him. This was a new one.

When everyone was back on four paws and looking the right way, I started the lead dogs down the road again. Slowly, I dropped back along the team as before. This time, however, I gripped the tuglines behind each pair of dogs as I walked with them. I helped pull a little, encouraging them forward as I did so. This seemed to work very well.

Several of the dogs even got the idea of basic dog mushing. Then the lead dogs ran around to the sled just as I reached it. Randolph again tangled two of his neighbors, this time including sweet Taffy, who couldn't stand the confusion and cried a lot.

The dragging of the lead dogs, the slow recession toward the sled, the lead dogs running back, Randolph doing his bit—all was repeated over and over.

I collapsed on the sled, weighted down by a heavy parka and twenty-seven years of existence.

There, by the bridge, one mile and four hours from the start, a sudden Truth came to me.

I took three swigs of cold water from the Thermos, stood up, and said to the world in general, "He who mushes dogs is crazy!"

It is a credit to my keen powers of observation that

I was able, after four hours of mushing, to make so final a statement. It has since stood the test of time. I even asked other mushers. One said it took him nearly forty years to learn it, but they all agreed.

I began again, the second mile taking only two hours. The same mishaps occurred, albeit with less frequency, on this stretch of ice and gravel.

About the thirty-seventh time I stooped to untangle Randolph, I arrived at a carefully thought-out plan. Standing up, I shouted:

"Wolves! You there, McKinley Park wolves! I realize how hungry you must be. I know how tough life is for you with all those Cessna 180's and double-ought buck and all! For you, as a present from good ol' Slim, I present you with eight warm meals! Come and gobble them up! Savor their stringy toughness! Rejoice in their succulent nastiness!"

Maybe huskies understand English. Some think they do. Maybe it was the tone of voice. That theory has its supporters. For all I know, the dogs can read lips, but all of a sudden the lead dogs remembered an appointment they had in Anchorage and started in that direction, quickly followed by six others. They looked nervously over their shoulders at me as they trotted off. Randolph trotted on ahead with a careful step to avoid tangling anyone, and the sled soon found that someone had thought-fully deposited two inches of hard-packed snow on the ground to ease its gliding.

For the first time in two miles, I stepped aboard the runners, cracked the whip, and yelled "On King!"

One hour later, we pulled into the dog yard of Bill and Ree Nancarrow at Deneki Lakes, and I tied the team to a truck.

Stumbling toward the house, ten miles from the start, I was admitted by Ree, who had promised me a cup of coffee when I would pass there.

Life behind a desk was telling on me. I asked to lie down for a minute, and promptly passed out. Several hours later I awoke to a bowl of hot soup.

Ree looked at me strangely for a minute, then said, "Slim, you've frostbitten your ear."

I touched my right ear, but she pointed toward the left one. When I touched that, it seemed that someone had pressed a hot iron against it. It was badly swollen, and hurt like hell.

How one ear froze with the other one untouched is still a mystery. My parka hood was down for most of the day, but the wind blew from directly behind me. By all rights, they both should have been frozen. It wasn't serious, of course, but there are always frostbite's lasting qualities to consider. Once a part has frozen, it will be prone to freeze more quickly than other parts for the lifetime of the bearer.

After my soup, I decided to continue down the road as far as I could before nightfall. I was still seventeen miles short of my projected day's trip to Cantwell, and felt I should keep going.

The dogs responded well, and we ran another four miles down to where Carlo Creek crossed the road. I picketed the dogs and had them fed when Bill Nancarrow drove up in the truck. His invitation to a hot meal and a bed was quickly accepted, and we drove back together.

I phoned in my story from Ree's sister's house nearby, and then enjoyed an evening with Bill and Ree and their two sons.

Bill had worked as a carpenter for the park for many years and was an accomplished musher. They operated their own silk screen business from their basement. Ree's art work and Bill's silk-screening of Alaskan Christmas cards is well known in this state. Ree also had a small team of dogs that she would run in the surrounding bush.

"Slim," Bill said, "you really ought to take some snowshoes with you for deep snow."

I laughed.

"Naw," I said, "there isn't enough snow to worry about, and they'd just take up room."

"You ought to, just the same," he said.

37

7

The dogs were anxious to see us the following morning when Bill and I arrived at Carlo Creek.

The amazing thing was that they seemed to like seeing me. After all the cussing and cuffing of the previous day, smiles were everywhere.

I slipped each one a doggy vitamin and harnessed them while watching Bill Nancarrow work. Bill, who had mushed more dogs through the Alaska Range than I had ever seen, was unloading the clumsy lump of frozen gear from the small sled basket, and sorting it out.

He shook his head and grinned.

"You've got a real problem here," he said, "about 150 pounds to carry on a sled designed to run empty."

We then went through the items one piece at a time, setting the heaviest toward the rear, the lighter to the front.

"In a racing sled," Bill said, "you have to keep the center of gravity to the rear. You've only got a little three-foot basket in this rig, so you have to be scientific about the whole thing."

Bill took the sheet of green plastic, stretched it over the empty sled, and began putting the heavy objects, like the fifty pounds of dog food, in the rear. Then the duffel bag went on top of that, with the light sleeping bag up in the front on the brush bow (the sled's curved bumper).

Bill then folded the remainder of the green plastic over the top of the load, lashing it together and to the sled with light rope.

This left only the short whip, the rifle, the dog food bucket, and the heavy picket chain. Where these could be placed on that full load, I couldn't have guessed.

While I stretched the towline to the front and began to snap the dogs to the rigging, Bill was solving the mystery. He slipped the Winchester Model 70 rifle through the lashing, with the butt in front of the musher within easy reach.

He then tied the whip (good mushers use whips only for their noise value) to the driving bow (the handle bars of the sled), and lashed the pail to the top of the load, open end up. To finish the job, he placed the thirty-pound picket chain in the bucket.

After a warm handshake, we said goodbye and

the dogs started down the road toward Windy Gap.

The difference Bill's "scientific" packing made in the sled's riding performance was amazing. There still wasn't enough snow to afford an easy glide to the sled, but it waggled through the icy gravel less than it had before.

The dogs by now had the idea of sledding in their heads, but the drag over gravel made it a heavy load. I walked along behind the runners, reaching ahead occasionally to straighten up the sled's path, or to aim it toward an icy patch. When the sled hit the ice, it would slip down low and smooth and glide. The dogs responded with a spurt of smooth pulling.

These patches would last only a few feet, and then we would be back on the gravel. Loose gravel would have been bad enough, but Alaska's winter version is worse. The Chinook had melted all the top snow, sending water running around the small rocks. When the freeze hit, the exposed pebbles were locked in place by frozen catches. The result was Alaskan sandpaper, and it was nearly fatal to the little sled.

A mile short of Windy Gap, with a north wind blowing down our necks, the wood creaked, the babiche lacing slipped, and one runner snapped its stanchions like a rifle shot and leaned crazily out into the road.

40

I stopped and gave the dogs a breather while I surveyed the damage. The wooden uprights had rotted enough over the years that they finally gave up their claims to the runner.

I had no tools to work with, and no patching materials but a length of clothesline rope. Winding the rope around the runner, I fastened it to the brake pedal rather roughly. The work went slowly. I had to remove my gloves to use my fingers. Then I had to put those freezing fingers back into the gloves for a thawing period.

During this time, the dogs curled up asleep in the harness and the wind blew ruffles in the fur on their backs. This habit of sleeping at the halt is common to all sled dogs, and my huskies fell into it by virtue of inheritance. The lone holdout was Jeff, the brown coon hound with the short hair who never could make the transition from treeing varmints to pulling one who stood on sled runners. Jeff just hopped around on cold feet and cried a lot.

When the lashing finally was done to my satisfaction, I fired up the team by hollering, and we went ahead. Nearly twenty feet. The sandpaper road carved through the rope quicker than I had expected and the runner again swung free.

By this time I was cold, mad, and thoroughly frustrated. The friendliness of the dogs in this situation made me even madder.

Sitting down on the collapsed sled, I took some time to think. I was about seven miles from Nancarrow's house, and about ten miles from Cantwell. Ahead lay Windy Gap, and I knew all the snow would be gone from the road there. The spot wasn't named on a whim.

Without tools and some baling wire, I would be all year limping with that broken sled into Cantwell. As I saw it, the best thing to do would be to walk into Cantwell and try to find some help. Not much choice, but it seemed better than sitting out there on the road.

Picketing the dogs to some spruces alongside the road, I pushed the sled over to the edge of the chain, and began walking to Cantwell.

The wind velocity in the upper Nenana River basin increases geometrically with each step taken toward Windy Gap.

Windy is the neck of the fastest bottle of wind in the North. Railroad men tell passengers that if all the wind in the world went suddenly calm, it would still blow hard and heavy through Windy Gap. They have good reason to feel this way, too. The railroad at one time built a section house along the tracks at the gap. The paint hadn't even dried on the house before the wind decided to change the design somewhat, and blew the roof one-hundred feet to a bunch of spruce trees.

The railroad took the hint, and has since moved

the section house, leaving Windy Gap to the winds.

Entering the narrow gap in a nearly horizontal position, I heard a car horn blow. There beside me was a station wagon containing two men and a pile of camping gear. They drove me cheerfully to Cantwell, but there was an embarassed manner about them that I didn't understand.

When they dropped me at the service station, the attendant cleared up the mystery by whispering, "That's the two guys with the dog team at the Healy tunnel . . ."

Those particular gentlemen, whose fame had spread for the entire length of the railroad by now, were the direct cause of a feeling that plagued me for weeks afterward. Their story, and a similar tale, deserve a telling of their own:

PARANOIA

Now Doc, I tell you these nightmares of being caught on the tracks by a fast freight have absolutely nothing to do with my sex life. Except of course, that if I'm ever caught out there by The Big Headlight, I won't have any more sex life.

No, Doc, the truth is, I heard a story from the conductor on the way to McKinley about an incident at the Healy Tunnel just a few miles north of where I started the sled trip.

It seems a track patrolman driving a gas car came out of

43

the darkness of the tunnel and immediately reversed his wheel spin and slid to a stop.

There, ahead of him, was a sled dog tied to the tracks. In fact, an entire team was tied to the tracks near the tunnel entrance.

The patrolman looked up the hill at two men by a campfire.

"What the hell are you doing here?" he said.

"Having breakfast," came the reply, "want some coffee?"

"Are you nuts? I'm only fifteen minutes ahead of a freight!"

Well, Doc, that interrupted their breakfast long enough to move the dogs off the tracks, and has interrupted my dreams ever since. The incident occurred one day before I started my trip.

Nor was that all, Doctor, because the main cause for my trauma occurred several years before that.

At that time a dog musher just outside Anchorage was running a team down the tracks when a freight came up behind him.

Now it takes those boys something like half a mile to stop a freight train when its rolling, and this one was gettin' with it.

The musher had his parka hood up and didn't hear the engine nor the whistle, until the last moment.

He jumped free, but the train took the sled and all six dogs with it.

44

So you see, Doc, that's what causes these awful dreams, and I've just got to do something about them.

What? Run the dogs on the highway from now on?

Why, Doc, didn't you hear about the time this big semi was coming up behind a musher on the Taylor Highway, and . . .

8

In Cantwell, there were eight businesses, seven of them under the same roof. Only the service station remained independent and aloof, a full fifty feet away from the others. The one roof shelters the store (hardware and grocery)-cafe-bar-news center-laundromat-public showers. And it sometimes serves as headquarters for a guide service.

Six months after my visit, I diversified the premises by bringing Cantwell's first library up to be stored in the building.

After making inquiries, I was sent to meet Henry Peters, an Athabascan Indian of about 50, who lived alone in his tarpaper cabin. I explained my plight, and Henry agreed to drive down and pick up the dogs and the broken sled.

We retrieved them and returned to Cantwell.

Peters spoke quite adamantly about the Native Land Claims Bill, then being considered in Congress. (It became law in the fall of 1971.)

"Naturally," he said, "being a Native, I'm all for it." (In Alaska, all Eskimos, Aleuts, and Indians are known under the respectful title of Natives. Helps eliminate tribal rivalry.)

According to him, the Bureau of Indian Affairs had promised schools for the Indian people of the Interior twenty years ago, and have never produced them.

In fact, even now, most Native children over 12, and many just six years old, must be flown to Mt. Edgecumbe School (near Sitka), some 2,000 miles away from their families.

Picture the kindergarten children in Denver being flown to San Francisco, put in a dormitory, and enrolled in school, and you have the general idea. Add language barrier to this situation, and real complications arise.

Cantwell, Henry Peters said, had been promised a high school years ago, and adult education had also been pledged. It still hasn't come about. "Perhaps if the Native people can have some money to spend, they will see that the little ones get some schooling."

Henry went to school through the eighth grade,

and then worked at hunting and trapping until the game was depleted.

"The white man came in with airplanes and killed most of the game around here," he said. "If you don't have an airplane, you don't stand much of a chance of even finding a caribou around here, let alone shooting one."

When Henry came of age, he went to work for the railroad as a laborer. He is still employed in that capacity.

Peters, as most men of his age in Alaska, had mushed dogs as a way of life in earlier years. His tips were valuable.

One of my bugaboos had been the choosing of a lead dog.

"Watch them all very carefully," Henry told me, "and you will find one dog that seems to go faster and act smarter than the others. Put him up front. When you get the right dog in the lead, the whole team will know it, and then you'll get the work from them."

As we neared Cantwell, the snow deepened, and in the little town, itself, there was a smooth-running four inches of hardpack on the plowed roadway—a real blessing.

"You should have good snow from here south," said Henry as we unloaded the sled at the gas station. "It will probably get deeper until you reach

48

Hurricane.   Watch for bad drifts near Broad Pass, though, if you stay on the road."

I thanked him for the ride and the advice, chained the dogs out of the way, and began to work on the sled.

There are lots of things that I can't do in this world, but the one thing I can't do even more than anything else is fix something that's broken.

To my aid came Larry Clark, a bush pilot and guide, who lived with his wife and baby about twenty miles from Cantwell.   They regularly flew to "town" to do the laundry and pick up supplies. Sometimes they flew back up with a hunter or fisherman.

With Larry's help, a hammer and some wire, the sled was soon ready for the trail.

By this time it was late afternoon and the sun had gone.

During dinner in the cafe portion of The Business, I thought about the day's lousy progress.   The dogs were fresh, having only mushed a few miles before the breakdown.   The snow was beautiful, and I learned the road to Summit was plowed all the way.   Summit is an F.A.A. flight service and weather station, 16 miles from Cantwell.

And a huge full moon was coming up over the Denali Highway to the east.

The phone service is pretty bad for people in

49

Cantwell. When I finally got the paper, I had to yell in my story. "I'M IN CANTWELL!"

"So am I!" yelled a drunk walking down the street.

I loaded the sled, and soon found I had lots of help with the dogs. As in any Native village, there was soon a number of children hanging around, holding fingers on bow knots, being dragged by huskies, and generally begging for a ride.

When all was loaded and harnessed, each of the kids had a ride up and down the street, except for one very quiet boy, who hung quietly back and hadn't asked for a ride.

"How about you?" I asked.

"I have to go to my grandfather's now," he said.

"Where does he live?"

"Down the road some."

"Hop on and let's go together."

Ronnie Pedro, 7, citizen of Cantwell, stepped on the runners and automatically shoved the brake into the snow.

"I'll hold them while you line 'em out!" he yelled with a grin.

The dogs started down the road slowly, with Ronnie riding the brake. I ran back and jumped on behind the boy, and he immediately released the brake and hollered, "Hy-a-a-ah!"

The dogs broke into a run for the first time, and

we clipped through the moonlight together, occasionally exchanging smiles. Once he looked back and said, "Pretty good team."

I swelled with pride at the compliment and said, "It's nothin' kid, when you know how to train 'em right."

Just then a dog barked off to the right at one of the houses, and his challenge was answered by eight dogs swerving up a snow berm in that direction, tangling themselves in deep snow and overturning the sled.

"Heh, heh," I said, smiling, "just one of their jokes."

He didn't seem too impressed, especially since I was sitting on his chest in a snowbank.

After five minutes of unravelling tuglines and the towline, kicking dogs, and shouting various ingenious nicknames for the leaders (I was trying Red and Randolph up front), we were back on the road.

This time, however, there was no compliment on the team from my assistant. In fact, he didn't even seem surprised at what happened when another dog barked on the other side of the road.

When I located Ronnie in the snowdrift beneath the overturned sled, he was in the third grade atomic attack position with hands laced over his head, his

51

head between his knees, and all sharp objects carefully removed from his pockets.

When would this dog-filled village end?

Two more charges of the harness brigade and we pulled up in front of a log cabin where the boy was staying.

Ronnie gave me a handshake such as a kamikaze pilot must have received before his first mission.

"Thank you for the ride," he said. "It was very interesting."

9

The road to Summit left the Denali Highway just beyond the boy's home, and the leaders swung out onto a broad, plowed racetrack of a road.

The road passes through a land of nearly treeless tundra. A wide valley, cut by glaciers and the Nenana River, slides smoothly through the divide in the Alaska Range. Just past Summit, a sign tells train passengers that Broad Pass is the lowest pass used by a railroad through the Rocky Mountains.

But physical descriptions fall woefully short of what I experienced that cold night.

Before leaving Anchorage, mushers had advised me that "They (the dogs) love to run at night, and you'll have fewer problems with them."

With no squabbles or tangles, the team leaped into the tugs. We loped along for about four miles before they settled into a fast "freight trot" for the rest of the 16 miles.

On my right, the Alaska Range sloped sharply up to peaks wrapped in a thin shroud of mist. To the left, the snowfield slipped in an unbroken frosting to a thin line of willows which marked a creek. Far beyond, the craggy mountains held snow and sheep and secrets.

The air was still, the moon was full, and to the north, a wispy opalescent ribbon of the Aurora Borealis began a stately swirling dance.

From time to time I would yell encouragement to the dogs, but they didn't need it.

I did.

I needed reassurance that the scene had some man-made part to it. The opposite of a guest walking past mountain murals in a hotel lobby (painted to remind city people that mountains still exist), I shouted to the team to break the atavistic hush.

Forgetting what nervousness I had about the dogs, I stood on both runners, my hood pulled over my head, and let my breath coat my beard with ice.

The sled glided smoothly, the soft crunching of snow beneath the runners the only noise. Ahead, eight dogs pulled steadily for the sheer joy of living, with no destination in mind. Ghostlike beneath the moon, the team pulled straight out, and me the sole passenger in the spectre procession.

54

I mumbled a silent prayer of thanks for being introduced to the rare beauty of a musher's night.

Almost in answer, the team stopped short and looked down toward the stream.

A low grumbling rose to a quivering howl as a prowling wolf protested our passage through his territory. We listened quietly for a minute, and then I just said "Hike," in a normal tone of voice, and Red lunged back into the lead. Again we sailed through a sea of snow.

Several miles short of the station, the cold night finally found its way into my parka, and I was chilled completely.

We pulled into the row of government buildings, and I picketed the dogs quickly to a loading platform. The temperature read minus twenty on a nearby building. My side was beginning to ache, and my left foot was raw with blisters.

I fed the dogs, and stumbled toward the nearest house. My only thought was to escape the cold for a few minutes. The steady drone of a diesel generator played a strange accompaniment to the dying flickers of the Northern Lights.

I took one last look at the night scene, saw the moon go behind some encircling clouds, and knocked on the door.

10

Being welcomed into a warm friendly kitchen after chaining dogs in snow eight feet deep is one of the nicest experiences available to man.

Abe and Nancy Wilson were just finishing a card game with their neighbor, George Gobel, when I came in.

Their two-year-old son was alternately dashing around and being shy in only a T-shirt.

Chilled and tired from the run through the night, I couldn't tell them more than my name until two cups of coffee had begun to work. Before I knew it, Abe was pulling off my mukluks, and running a hot bath for me.

Nancy made up the spare bed, and George was cheering me up with jokes. The modern lights, oil heat, and stereo music seemed totally out of synch with the outside world. But still, the warmth of the peoples' voices and the majesty of the outdoors were part of Alaska.

While bathing, I checked my foot only to find large areas of skin rubbed off by sweaty socks. Socks must be changed daily in extreme cold. With activity, the foot sweats, soaking the socks. When the foot rests (as while riding the sled runners), the socks crust with ice and oil from the skin and form an abrasive. I had worn these socks two days in a row. I wouldn't make that mistake again.

Refreshed from the bath, I found my host a very interesting man.

Now in his twenties, Abe had decided while still in school to break the poverty mold that holds so many of the Indian people in his home village of Nondalton near Lake Iliamna.

He explained the troubles he had had earlier in locating the job he now holds as a trainee in the weather station at Summit:

"When I applied to the B.I.A. for aid in learning this trade," he said, "I was refused. They said they didn't have funds for that type of program. The woman who told me this had taught school in Nondalton, so I began to tell her the names of all the people there who were being 'paid' by the B.I.A. to sit home and drink. She knew the people and knew

I wasn't lying, so she 'found' the money somewhere for me to go to school."

He went to school, and several months later, the Wilson family was warmly housed in their two-bedroom home in Summit.

During the day, Abe worked in the nearby tower, taking readings on temperature, humidity, snowfall, wind direction, and wind velocity. When I visited the tower early the next morning, I found the area full of equipment and score sheets. The Summit Flight Service Station is a necessary aid to navigation of all aircraft flying the pass between Anchorage and Fairbanks.

Higher up, the trans-polar jets get aid in weather information and the latest predictions.

Abe works with an intensity understood only by someone who has lived daily with poverty and hunger. He found his way out, and is vocal about it.

"I don't care," he said to me, "if the Native people get $10,000 each in the claims settlement (they didn't) or if we get nothing. I consider myself an American and have opportunities to learn the same as anyone."

As Algerish as his attitude sounds, however, Abe occasionally finds holes in his own arguments. He attended an "Indian school" in Oregon, free of charge, because he is an Indian. His job training came about, too, because of his membership in a minority race.

"Still," he adds, "the Native people from my area have to realize that they must keep up with society and adapt to civilization."

But arguments were far from my thoughts as I started down the facility's driveway on the morning of what was to become my most difficult and painful day on trail.

11

The dogs were feeling fit as they plunged into a run down the road. Never had my spirits been so high. The dogs had become a team, and my body, despite its many aches and pains, started to shake off the effects of the desk, and become a little more wiry as the days passed.

The road from Summit to Broad Pass had been built several years before, and two years later it became a part of the Anchorage–Fairbanks Highway. Now, however, only the first mile south of Summit was plowed, leaving the remaining ten miles to the whims of Nature.

We jogged along at our customary trot on the road paralleling the railroad tracks, and separated from them by several hundred yards.

Those tracks!

I looked with scorn and fear at them there, off to

my left. On those tracks run big trains that hurt dogs and mushers. I was on the road, the good old road. No trains, no gas cars, no over-the-shoulder paranoia.

Then the snowmachine track we'd been following down the unplowed road stopped, and the team faced an unbroken ridge of snow about two feet high.

The dogs halted, and the leaders (I was trying Taffy and Shep up front) ran back for moral support.

Randolph did a *demi plie* with a half-gainer, and the entire team was hog-tied. He was becoming proficient at his hobby.

After unravelling the yarn, I took the leaders back to the front and walked alongside to reassure them. It was about then that I encountered my first taste of one of Alaska's homegrown nightmares, the whiteout.

Whiteout is a cessation of depth perception, and damn near every other kind of perception, caused by a certain combination of snow cover, cloud cover, and diffused light from the snow.

All at once, there is no horizon. Snow and sky are the same, and the whole world becomes an off-white. No shadows aid in navigation, and without the keener sense of the dogs for help, a man could walk or drive a snowmachine right off a cliff.

A North Slope helicopter pilot told me how he

had been caught suddenly in a whiteout about five miles from camp. He landed, and, through compass bearings, sent a passenger ahead on foot about one-hundred feet—the limit of visibility at the time. He would then fly the chopper up to where the man was, and wait until he had walked another hundred feet. This continued until camp was reached . . . five hours later.

Now I was in a fix. All I could see was a huge blanket of snow, and the dogs.

My dark goggles did nothing to relieve this. The only thing to do was to sit down and have a cup of coffee.

Not having coffee, I just sat down.

Further travel on the road was slow and agonizing. The unplowed surface was deep, and nothing warned a man when he left it, except that he sank into about six feet of soft powder. The only other visible thing was the telephone poles and railroad tracks one-hundred yards to the left.

"I can make that easily," I thought. "A paltry hundred yards. The length of a football field. The distance of a dash. I once did that in under 12 seconds. No sweat, just run across there and whip onto those tracks. I know the snow is only about six inches deep between the rails, and I can take a few looks over my shoulder for any trains."

With all my spirits gathered, I awakened the team from their coffee break, and swung the leaders out onto the soft snow.

Immediately, I fell into snow up to my armpits and cussed myself for not taking Bill Nancarrow's snowshoes along. Carving steps in the far wall of the pit, I stepped up onto the surface, and plunged down again, dragging the leaders a few feet with me as I went.

This time I would be smart. I would crawl on hands and knees when I came out of my pit.

Again I stomped steps in the wall, and this time I went into a crawl position.

The pit was wider as I sank down on all fours through the snow.

From my position in the hole, I pulled the dogs hand-over-hand past me, to get them as far toward the tracks as I could.

The leaders began whimpering and crying, and soon all eight of them were bawling.

Out of frustration, Nameless began a fight, and Randolph panicked, lacing everyone into a tightly-knit group. Floundering through the drifts, I hammered on Nameless, taking an accidental bite on the hand as I did so.

Twenty minutes later, the team was untangled and floundering in the drifts. The sharp pain in my left side, which I had first noticed the day before, had become a knife, and my breathing was labored.

We struggled forward, repeating the same hole-and-cut-steps procedure, until we had gained another ten feet. When the sled finally left the road for the deep snow, it pitched over on its side.

With tears of frustration, I waded back and righted it, then began my journey back to the lead dogs.

By this time, I was swearing at not only my stupidity about the snowshoes, but at the world in general, dog mushing in particular, and the Alaskan outdoors specifically.

The lead dogs would be dragged forward a few feet, then the unwieldy sled would flop over on its side. Once the trip to the sled was made, I would go in and out of my previous holes to the leaders, dragging them until the sled flopped again.

After about the third trip back to the sled, the pain in my chest became so unbearable that I had only the use of my right arm. The left could only be held straight down at my side.

Heavy, warm clothing doesn't help in a situation like this, and when we had struggled about half the distance to the tracks, I was completely out of breath, and gasping after only thirty seconds of effort.

Then Nature found relief.

As I was trying to straighten the sled, the dogs surged forward, running the sled over my chest and pressing me deep into the snow.

Pushing as hard as I was able against the sled, my strength began to weaken.   The sounds around me grew faint, and I slipped into darkness.

When I awoke, my watch told me I had been unconscious for fifty minutes.   Red's tongue was working my face over, and he stood astraddle of me, growling occasionally when the others drew too close.   Four of the dogs were looking down at me curiously.

Red was whimpering.   Randolph had one of his legs securely fastened to Taffy's white tail, but still wore his irrepressible grin.

"Well boys," I said, "looks like we're in a hell of a fix, doesn't it."

Taffy wagged her tail and Randolph's leg.

I was thinking clearly now, and realized that it would be easier to tunnel out from beneath the sled than to try and push it away from me.   In a few minutes, I was free.

Slowly and methodically, I pulled up the sled with my good hand and untangled the dogs.   I kept reminding myself to go slowly.

The dogs covered the remaining distance to the tracks in the same fashion as before, but now they had settled down to business.   After four hours of struggle, I pulled the sled up between the tracks, and lay thankfully down across the runners. The broken trail through the snow behind us looked as though it had been bombed.

At that point, I would have waved cheerfully at a freight as it ran over us, but fortunately none was due.

Hearing the sound of a plane, I watched Larry Clark's Super Cub flying low down the tracks. I raised one arm to signal "Okay," and he waggled his wings and flew home. I couldn't have held both arms up to signal for help if I needed it.

The pain in my side stayed with me for the remainder of the trip, but was never again as bad as it was that day. The doctor eventually diagnosed it as an inflamed rib cartilage, and advised me not to lift anything heavier than five-hundred pounds for a week or so. It hasn't bothered me since.

The dogs, once they had rested, lined out in front of the sled in their jog trot, and I watched the telephone poles go by.

A strong light came into view around a bend, and a few minutes later, Jack Burton was helping me chain the dogs at the Broad Pass section house.

Somewhere in that tortuous run between Summit and Broad Pass, we had crossed the Continental Divide, and were now headed downhill toward Anchorage.

12

Jack Burton, his family, and a laborer named Clarence were the only residents of Broad Pass.

They lived in one of the yellow and brown section houses built by the railroad at twenty-five to thirty-mile intervals for the men who make minor repairs on the track.

Mrs. Burton invited me for dinner, and I called the office with my story. The paper told me I was to call a television station in Anchorage and give them a story also each day. They taped the phone conversation, and played it back later on the news. It seemed strange to be able to talk to thousands of people over the telephone at Broad Pass.

I bunked that night in the bachelor's quarters with Clarence. We drank a lot of coffee and talked dogs, snowshoes, and winter travel long into the night.

67

Clarence, an Indian from the Kenai Peninsula, had run his share of dogs in his youth.

The day dawned crisp and clear, and I was eager to get started. At six each morning at the section houses, everyone on the tracks picks up the phone and gets the daily line-up of trains from the dispatcher. The line-up tells each person along the railroad when to expect each train. Every section foreman knows within a few minutes about how long it takes each train to reach his area, and can arrange to have his gas car off on a siding when the train goes through.

Every morning after that, while having breakfast with the section foreman's family, I would be given a list of the trains. By calculating the speed of my team for the day, he could tell me when to start "looking over my shoulder" for each train. None of these calculations by the railroad people were more than five minutes off for the entire trip.

The dogs gave me the usual early morning troubles. For the first short distance each day, they felt obliged to pick fights, get tangled, chase rabbits, cry a lot, and relieve themselves. The "trouble stretch," as I called it, gradually shortened during the trip, until finally only the first hundred yards was chaos.

We had just finished the trouble stretch that morning. The weather was overcast but rather nice:

temperatures in the mid-twenties, and perfect mushing between the rails.

All of a sudden, one of the dogs lunged off the tracks, followed by the entire team. Fights began, and white things were being tugged at, fought over, and thrown into the air.

The dogs had come across an entire covey of willow ptarmigan that had probably flown into the train and been killed. The dead birds were strung along the tracks for better than a hundred yards. Alaska's state bird, the ptarmigan is all white in winter except for a few black tail feathers. They resemble quail, but are slightly larger.

Finding it impossible to dislodge any of the birds from the mouths of the stronger dogs, I picked up some more birds and handed them out to the crew. With a bird in every mouth, we marched off down the tracks toward the flats at Colorado.

After seven miles of rolling woodland and lakes, we arrived. Once a section station on the railroad, Colorado now consists of an empty trapper's cabin and a sign.

After a smoke break for me, and a ptarmigan-eating break for the dogs, we continued down the tracks to Honolulu, and ate lunch. Honolulu, once widely-known as a trapping center, is now just a long siding and a sign. It is the halfway point between Anchorage and Fairbanks, and the passenger trains meet and pass there during the summer schedule. The sign at Honolulu was barely visible through eight-foot drifts of snow, and I shot a picture of it. Later, I chuckled to think that I had driven a dog team from Colorado to Honolulu in about an hour. Thor Heyerdahl, please take note.

A southbound freight passed us during our lunch break, and slowed enough to ask if we were all right and needed anything. I waved him on gratefully. By this time, everyone on the Alaska Railroad knew about the trip, and the trains would slow down and begin blowing their whistles several miles from me. Officially, of course, I was not supposed to be on the tracks, but they overlooked it in the spirit of the trip.

Miles later, I arrived at the north end of the Hurricane Gulch bridge. This chasm, impressive from the passenger car on the moose gooser, is terrifying on foot. The trestle stretches over four-hundred yards to the opposite bank, and two-hundred ninety-six feet down is a thin silver streak known as Hurricane Creek. Downstream about two miles, Hurricane Creek empties into the great Chulitna River.

The southbound passenger train was due in fifteen minutes, and I did not consider that ample time to cross, so I pulled the dogs off the tracks and lit my pipe.

70

I didn't have much of a wait. The train could be heard laboring up the steep grade we had just climbed, and the engineer blew the whistle several times to warn me (and any wayward moose on the trestle) that he was approaching.

In winter, the train usually consists of about four cars and half-a-dozen locals riding to town to get supplies (or drunk). This day it was different, however. The train slowed down as it always does at the trestle, and people began to pop out of the spaces between the cars with cameras and take pictures of us, yelling "Hi Slim!" and waving. After six hours of mushing dogs through steep canyons with no sound except the ice-choked rivers, those friendly voices picked up my spirits. Even the dogs seemed happier.

Then the train began its slow crawl across the high span like a tightrope-walking snake. The flashing red light on the rear car finally swung around the bend in the trees and disappeared, like the quivering rattle of a surprised snake.

Now I was home free. I knew that there were no more trains scheduled until a northbound freight passed in about five hours. By that time, I would be sound asleep at Hurricane section house (four miles south of the gorge).

To my surprise, the Hurricane trestle was the easiest trestle to cross on the entire railroad. The ties had been planked over so that moose using the bridge couldn't catch a leg between the ties and derail a train. The dizzy depths of that canyon made it plain a train would only be derailed once at that spot.

Not pressed for time, I got out the camera and fooled around a little, taking pictures of the team against the sign, then leading the dogs out onto the trestle and taking pictures of them peering over the edge. They didn't enjoy the view any more than I did.

Slowly we made our way out to the center of the bridge. In the center, with two hundred yards to go, I stopped the team for more pictures.

Then all my nightmares bore fruit.

From behind us to the north came a pair of headlights. I jumped and waved and yelled, but still they came. At that section of the trestle, there is no place to go unless you have a parachute and lots of life insurance.

Finally, the car (a station wagon mounted on train wheels) blinked its lights in recognition, and slowed down to let me cross. I didn't waste any time in getting the dogs across the trestle. At the south end, I pulled the team off the tracks and went over to apologize to the men. They were I. P. Cook and Jack Church (two honchos from the railroad), and I could picture eight dogs and a musher spending time

72

in Leavenworth for a trespass violation. As it turned out, they knew about where I was, and were friendly, and we drank some coffee. They took some film in to the office for me. Then they shook hands and left. I just shook.

The remaining four miles to Hurricane section house were driven in the dark, and I was very tired. The dogs seemed to drag, too, and a slow walk was all I could get out of them. Feeling sorry for them, I pushed the sled and yelled encouragement, but each step they took seemed to be an agony, and they groaned with exhaustion.

I sure felt sorry for them. It had been a long 30 miles for me, too, but still I helped them the best I could.

Then (please pay attention, all bleeding hearts) the boys spotted the porch light on the section house about a mile away, and heard Ed Schweitzer's dog barking in the yard.

I managed to grab the driving bow of the sled and pull myself onto the runners as we streaked down the tracks at twenty miles per hour. Swearing loudly at the three miles of pushing I had just completed, we swung into the yard at a good clip, and I condemned each guilty but happy face as I chained and fed them that night.

13

Ed Schweitzer, his lovely wife, and their six kids were good people. Mrs. Schweitzer, a Native Alaskan, cooked a fine moose roast, and showed me her classroom in the basement. It was furnished with regular school desks and a blackboard, and all but her youngest attend her school there daily. The youngest didn't attend only because he was too young. He looked forward to being in the classroom the following year. His name was Gopher.

There had been two narrow escapes for the Schweitzer family. Once, a helicopter struck the hundred-foot tower holding their radio antenna and crashed just yards from the house, killing the pilot and exploding.

On another occasion, fire destroyed an outbuilding and threatened the house. No one in the family was injured either time.

I fell asleep over dinner. Foggy impressions ran through my mind the following morning as the sled glided down a gentle slope toward Chulitna and the treacherous Indian River Canyon. I hoped "Gopher" was only a nickname for that little kid.

The Alaskan winter day felt bright and clear, although a light snow was falling. For an hour, the dogs trotted on down the tracks in the snow. The blowing snow sifting through the team made it seem as though the dogs were entering a tunnel. At times, only the wheel dogs were visible.

Then the snow cleared away and I came to Chulitna, with its beautiful lake and Mt. McKinley showing itself at its largest.

There is nothing at Chulitna but several cabins and the lake, but it has to be one of the prettiest places in Alaska. McKinley is only forty-six miles away (the closest the railroad comes to the giant 20,300-foot rock), and it overshadows the entire scene as though viewed through a telephoto lens.

The top of the mountain was experiencing high winds, which blew funnels of snow into the sky in a volcano-like mist.

We stopped for coffee and a snooze, then began the drop into the Indian River.

Indian River is a famous and beautiful grayling and Dolly Vanden stream in summer. In the winter, however, the waters of the river are cold, swift, and deadly. Its clear waters flow fast through a beautiful but narrow canyon crossed many times by the tracks. In fact, many trestles are so close together in places, it seemed they just reached across the river, grabbed a rock for support, then shot across the river again as it wound back under the bridge.

The old-timers have since told me that in the early days it was much colder up here than it is now for these city-bred cheechakoes, and in those days, they would just run down the ice on the river rather than taking a chance on the train tracks.

Unfortunately, however, these were modern days and the winter had been unusually mild, so that a stream of running water marked the middle of the ice-choked channel.

We couldn't even start to try that bad ice.

Ask a sled dog about a railroad trestle, and he'll howl with fright, later calming down enough to tell you that there is nothing worse in a dog's life. From the first step on a trestle, dogs feel that at any moment they will slip between the ties and plunge through space for forty-five seconds, and then be bitten by wolverines waiting at the bottom next to the porcupines.

76

It makes no difference how much distance there is between the tracks and the ground, either. A fall of three-hundred feet, or three feet—the dogs react identically. In fact, the easiest trestle was the Hurricane Bridge, by far the highest and scariest.

As we tried the trestles along Indian River, the distinct personality of each dog became more apparent.

Red would walk along the right-hand side of the rail on the short stubs of the ties rather than in the middle.

His partner, little Randolph, would tightrope-walk on top of the left rail until safely on the other side. Sometimes, Red would swerve to the right a little, pulling Randolph off his rail. He'd give Red a dirty look and hop right back up.

Shep had to be dragged over the first few trestles, but after that would walk slowly across with the others.

I can't recall anything of Jeff's trestle activities, so I imagine he didn't give much trouble and went along.

Nameless hated the trestles, and would start a fight with another dog at being made to cross each one. He would have to be thumped regularly at the start of each bridge.

Taffy cried a lot, and also had to be dragged, which was nothing new. She had decided early in the game that she had special privileges due her, and didn't pull a lick for the entire trip.

The one dog that finally took the initiative and began walking across trestles was Scarface, the battered white dog who looked as though he had gone through the Korean War—and lost. He began slowly, with his legs far apart much as a sky-diver would, and began eating up the railroad ties. This earned him the lead dog slot.

But it was Big John that caused all the trouble on the trestles. This 90-pound overstuffed toy Malemute would have a stroke at each trestle we came to. He was still in the "wheel" position, so I watched his antics close-up.

First, he would cry loudly. Then he would collapse with his head between his front paws and moan as if he were dying. Then, of course, the sled would run over his tail, causing him to leap and do spins in the air, punctuated with war whoops.

Then he discovered that he could line up with the center of the sled, go into his "prayers to Mecca" position, and have the sled go over his head. This pulled his collar over his head. With his head free, but still harnessed, he would race around the sled toward me, begging for mercy.

His final accomplishment was to lie down facing the same direction as the other dogs, and let their forward motion peel the harness over his head. He would daintily lift each front leg as the harness passed, freeing himself to run and accept congratulations on his good fortune.

Dragging a 90-pound dog someplace he didn't care to go was out of the question, so I was forced to carry him across.

I would take the team across (after he had freed himself), then return for John, hoist him to my shoulders, and pack him over.

On the second trestle we crossed in this fashion, I decided this had to cease. Right in the midst of carrying him across, along came lineman Dean Cook on a gas car. He laughed so hard at us that I couldn't hear what he said until we were across.

Big John began the trip in the "sheep carry" position in my arms, but decided that this position wasn't stable enough. He had then crawled around into a piggy-back position with his feet wrapped around my neck, his head hanging over my shoulder, looking down at the four-foot drop between the ties, his mouth open, crying every step.

When we reached the other side, and Cook had finished laughing, I told him of my problem and asked for suggestions. He came up with a good one.

The next trestle was only one-hundred yards away. I let John pull free of his collar and harness, and I crossed the trestle with the rest of the team. Instead of going back for him, though, I just kept on driving the team until we had gone out of sight around a bend in the trail. Then I stopped and waited.

If there is one thing a sled dog hates worse than trestles, it's solitude. John was going crazy. He wouldn't go down on the ice, I knew, because of the danger, and he couldn't go back, because of the trestle we had just crossed.

So he cried a lot, and ran back and forth at the north end of the bridge, while the team slept and I filled my pipe.

After fifteen minutes, John finally crossed the bridge, and came charging up to the sled as pleased as though he had just won the Fur Rendezvous weight pull.

I put him in harness and drove on. After that, I had a good team of trestle dogs. When the last trestle was crossed, several days later, I rode the runners across, and just yelled encouragement as they crossed.

A good Alaska Railroad trestle dog is hard to come by.

14

As we pulled out of the Indian River Canyon and back onto some straighter, flatter track, we rounded a bend and encountered a large work crew piling into gas cars to head for work after lunch. They were part of what is called an extra gang, which does the heavier repair work on the tracks. Their headquarters are a string of cars parked on a siding, and moved whenever the job is completed.

The men smiled and greeted me as I pulled up to the cars, and a few took pictures of the team. The foreman said, "If you're hungry, I imagine Opal would give you something to eat. Second car back." Thanking them, I cached the team off the tracks and walked back to the second car.

My plan was to be at the Canyon siding (where I was then) at two p.m. for some pictures to be taken from a plane containing reporters from the *Daily*

News. I had one hour (one lunch hour, that is) to kill.

I knocked on the door of the car.

"Thought you guys were working!"

"Uh, they are . . . ma'am . . ."

"Oh," she said, opening the door, "thought you were one of those worthless . . . well, come in . . . and scrape your feet, dammit!"

"Yes, ma'am."

Opal, I learned later, had been known to throw plates of food at anyone who would dare to even ask for extra salt on the food.

"You might as well eat, now you're here. . . . Hungry, I suppose? . . . Cold cuts will have to do, cause I sure ain't cookin' up something just for you. . . . These them dogs I heard about? . . . Kinda scroungy lookin' but I guess you can't expect more than that if you got 'em free. . . . How'd you work that? . . . Here, don't talk . . . eat . . . I ain't got all day to get these dishes done. . . ."

So I ate.

When I had finished, Opal poured two cups of coffee and sat down across from me. I was going to ask her how she liked being the only woman with a crew of about 15 men, but before I was able to:

"You're a writer-fella, so you are probably going to ask me how I like being the only woman out here

82

with all these mangy men . . . Well, I'll tell
you. . . . It   ain't   too   bad . . . mostly.
. . . I've been out here nearly twenty years
with one crew or another, cookin', cleanin' up
and just generally keepin' those crums from
dyin'. Honestly, how they remember to put on
their boots each day is . . . but anyway, you
probably want to know if they made any passes at
me and such . . . had another writer-fella in here
who did once . . . wanted to know, that is
. . . not made a pass . . . I meant the men
making a pass . . . you know. . . . Well, in
nearly twenty years they's only been one of them
crums ever made a pass at me . . . (she chewed on
her cigarette in a meaningful pause) . . . and he
damn near didn't survive it. It was many years
ago . . . I was lots prettier than now (she primped
her hair) . . . and this little mouse got tanked up
one night . . . sneaked a bottle of whiskey into
camp . . . you know . . . and he came up behind me while I was doing dishes and put his filthy
arms around me . . . the weasel! . . . So I turned
around and smashed him in the head with a skillet. . . . Damn near killed him . . . and I haven't
had no trouble with the boys since."

She spat into a can. Dead center.

"You know, my daddy always used to say that if a
girl always acts like a lady . . . men are going to

treat her like a lady . . . believed that now all these years . . . and it's always true . . . you gonna write that down? Don't matter . . . it's all true . . . the other writer-fella, he didn't write that . . . just a bunch of bull about me being the best cook on the railroad and such. . . . Can't say that I am . . . really . . . but you don't ever hear those guys complainin' about the food . . . the crums!"

I'll bet not, I agreed, and thanked her for the lunch.

"What are you gonna write about me? . . . Well, I guess I'm not supposed to ask . . . (Spit-tooey! . . . ding!) . . . you writer-fellas always think up something . . . don't you . . . and then WHAMMO! (I jumped back against the door) . . . the next thing you know, there it is in print . . . say, you don't talk much, do you? . . . Well, that's the way some people are . . . good to be that way, too . . . my old daddy used to say . . . well, that's another story . . . take care of them dogs, and don't let the men razz you about them none . . . the weasels!"

15

Visions of that flying skillet flashed through my brain as I chuckled and untangled the team. Opal could hardly be called typically Alaskan, but in a way she really is. Characters are the spices for the meat and potatoes living of bush life. If a man isn't a little strange, he's either a tourist, or he lives in Anchorage.

I drove the dogs down the tracks for about a mile, keeping an ear peeled for both the sound of an airplane engine, and the hum of a southbound freight which was due through in a few minutes.

The freight came first.

I pulled the team off the tracks, winding the leader up to where I could hold him, and grabbed the sled with the other hand. Then I heard the single engine of the light plane coming up the canyon . . . right on time.

Bill Fox was at the controls, with photographer Dennis Cowals and reporter Linda Billington alongside.

This is a nice note, I thought. Here they fly up from Anchorage to take dog mushing pictures, and I'm stuck in a snowbank holding the team. I was hoping they were high enough to see the oncoming freight and realize what I was doing there. They were, and circled until the train had passed.

Then we started out to give them a Sergeant Preston-type show. Amazingly, the dogs strung out and trotted nicely down the tracks. I cracked the little whip a few times for show, and Dennis immortalized us on celluloid from the plane.

After the plane made a few passes, it came low, waggled its wings, and Linda dropped a brown paper sack out of the plane. Now Linda's a fine reporter, a good dog musher, and real pretty, but she'd never make it in the Air Force. The bag sailed over our heads, landing in deep snow about one-hundred feet off the tracks.

Elated at receiving a present, I quickly took the team off the tracks, tied the leader to a rock (Shep and Scarface were running in front at that time), and went to see if I could find the package.

I had no snowshoes with me, and the snow was a good four feet deep. Before I had slogged half the distance to where I thought the package would be, I heard the fight.

86

The fight was fierce, but was over in about fifteen seconds.

I didn't think it could have been too serious, but forgot the package and returned to the dogs anyway.

Coming up the bank, I saw a team of dogs looking embarassed and ashamed. Lying helplessly where I had tied him was Scarface—stone dead and partially dismembered.

I sat down in the midst of the bloodied dogs and thought about it.

I could probably have "forgotten" the incident editorially, but then, I would have to come up with some white dog named Scarface at the finish, and explain to the honchos at the pound, and this was a web I didn't want to get tangled in.

As I sat there, I began to piece together the incident. Most of the dogs had blood on them. Shep, Scarface's partner in the lead, had blood on one foot, and the other one was cut slightly. Knowing him, however, these were probably the results of evasive action as the others were killing his partner.

Jeff began growling and chewing at the dead dog. I kicked him away, unharnessed the body, and buried it in a deep snowbank off the tracks. Later in the spring, when the ground thawed, track patrolman John Lewis buried the body properly.

One look at Nameless spelled out the beginnings of the battle. The position of leader had been

87

shared by every dog in the team except Big John at one time or another during the trip, as I tried to find which dog or dogs worked best there. Nameless had run lead for two days, before I discovered that Scarface was so much better at starting the team across trestles.

When Nameless had been removed from the favored spot and put in the wheel, his surliness increased. His fighting became more frequent. He was now standing within range of the dead dog's position, with blood and white hair on his muzzle. It didn't take a genius to learn who had started the fight.

Huskies are a gentle loving breed of dog when handled with decency and fairness. I have had perhaps thirty adult huskies since that trip, and have never owned one that I wouldn't trust with a baby. They are the worst watchdogs in the world, and would undoubtedly help a burglar pack the silverware off. They will, however, kill each other at times quite mercilessly and naturally.

House dogs in town keep to a battle plan. The fight begins with growled threats, lasts a few bites, the loser runs away howling, and the fight is over.

When huskies fight, they just fight. The attacker attempts to knock the opponent down. This is usually done by a feint, followed by a hard slam to the shoulder, rolling the dog over. The attacker then tears out the loser's throat. Unattended, a fight between sled dogs almost always results in a dead dog.

Some people may think that this trait derives from the huskies' close kinship to the wolf, but naturalists tell us that wolves don't fight each other to the death.

Scarface was no slouch in a brawl, however, and it was difficult to figure how he could have been dispatched in so short a fight.

Later, other mushers told me more of the huskies' fight strategy. The other dogs wait until one of the combatants is down and is clearly getting the rough end of it. Then they all pile on to "get a piece of the action," and proclaim fealty to the new leader.

This is undoubtedly what happened that afternoon, judging from the distribution of blood among the embarrassed group.

The only other logical choice for a lead dog at that point was old Nameless himself, although I was so mad at him I would have done most anything but give him the favored spot in the team. But he got it—and then a funny thing happened.

As soon as he took the lead, the rest followed faithfully, with a greater speed of trot than I had ever gotten out of them. Nameless, without a growl, curled his tail over his back, smiled, and took off down the tracks.

I recalled Henry Peters' remark about the leader,

"When the right dog takes the lead, you'll know it."

And so did the others. If I live to run dogs for fifty years, I'll never fathom the intricacies of their pecking order.

About one mile from the Gold Creek section house, and crossing a bridge over the Susitna River, we first met John Lewis in his gas car. John's job is to patrol the tracks from Chase in the south to Colorado in the north, about 75 miles, to be sure that nothing blocks the path of the trains.

Explaining the tragedy of the day to John, I included the location of the forgotten sack of goodies. Then we said goodbye and I started the team toward the porch light of the section house.

We pulled into the yard, warmly welcomed by Oscar, the section house dog, (we later found he was probably a relative of Randolph's) and I staked the dogs across the tracks and fed them. It had been a long day. Only nineteen miles, but the death of Scarface had stretched it into a miserable distance.

16

We had barely reached the yard before the section foreman, Don LaRose, came out to help with the dogs, adding an invitation for the night.

"You look like you need a drink," he said, "and I've got one with your name on it."

His wife, Florence, came out and stood quietly looking at the dogs. She looked a bit surprised, but it wasn't until later that night I was to learn why.

After dinner we were having a smoke when Florence's soft voice broke the quiet.

"Those are just regular dogs, Slim, aren't they?"

"I guess so," I said, not knowing exactly what she was getting at.

"Well," she answered, "I was looking in the paper at your stories, and you said they were green dogs. They all looked just brown and black and white to me."

But the early evening had been an emotional

catastrophe. During my phone call to the newspaper office, there had come a gasp from the rewrite man on the other end.

"Oh God!"

Then I heard him yell into the newsroom, "One of Slim's dogs got killed!"

There was a hustle around on the other end of the phone, and then my boss, Stan Abbott, came on the line.

"What happened?"

I told him.

"Okay. Whew! Wait until Larry (Fanning) hears this! Okay, just give us the story the way it happened, but we may sit on it a day or so, so don't say anything over the air tonight, okay?"

I agreed, gave the rewrite man the story, and hung up. On the call to the television station, I simply said that it had been a trying day, that Nameless had been put into the lead position again, and that we were then at Gold Creek.

Later, I learned of some of the confusion the story had caused at the newsroom. Linda Billington called other mushers, and learned that losing dogs to fighting was a common occurrence among them. The president of the S.P.C.A. was informed of the killing, and he was only worried about me being upset, and understood.

Larry then decided to run the story I had given, and it appeared verbatim in the morning edition, with a sidebar story from Linda on what she had learned from other mushers.

When the phone calls were over, there was a knock at the door, and John Lewis walked in with my paper sack. He had walked straight to it with snowshoes. Inside were news clippings of the trip, several extra dog harnesses, a pocket knife from my friend Lloyd Haessler, and a note from the staff.

Despite the pleasant company, I was in a bad mood that evening over the loss of that scroungy white dog. Don walked over with a drink, squeezed my shoulder, and told me to relax.

"Those things happen, Slim," he said. "There has never been an easy way to do anything in Alaska. Come on, let's play some music."

Don and Florence then brought out two electric guitars, and we began to play and sing. The whiskey warmed my insides, and the company warmed my thoughts.

Don is a long-time Alaskan, who came as a small boy during the migration of the 1930's, helping his parents homestead in what is now known as the "settler's acreage" around Palmer.

He grew up in the hard mold of a homesteader—building cabins, cutting firewood, clearing fields, and finally working for the Alaska Railroad. With his background, it is no surprise that LaRose ended up in a bush section house rather than an office in Anchorage.

Don's the kind of guy you could leave in the woods with only an ax, and when you came to get him in the spring, he'd have a warm meal, dry bed, and a cup of coffee waiting for you.

Florence has the quietest and sweetest voice I believe I've ever heard. Don is always talking about the glories of marrying an Eskimo woman, and Florence is the best kind of argument for that theory that I know.

Florence's parents were from Barrow, and left there at an early age with several other families to find a better place to live.

They traveled by foot, skin boat (oomiak), and dog team across the barren tundra of the Arctic Slope for hundreds of miles, finally entering Canada. For several months, they tried various areas in northern Canada, and then again migrated south and west into interior Alaska. They floated down the treacherous Porcupine River to Fort Yukon, where it joins the larger Yukon River. Eventually, they were shown hospitality by the Athabascan Indians in the village of Beaver, some seventy miles downstream on the big river, and made it their home. There Florence was born.

Not all of the people that started the trip finished at Beaver. A few stayed in villages along the way, and more than one rested permanently beneath rock cairns on the frozen slopes of the unforgiving Brooks Range.

94

17

From Gold Creek, the tracks wind gradually and slowly through the Susitna River Valley. They hug the east bank of the river, at times so closely that if a train were to come along, dogs and musher would find themselves on river ice.

The Susitna River is one of the most beautiful creations in this land. I love islands, and the big Su is full of them along this area. They range from less than one to more than five acres in size, are covered with large cottonwoods, and the river breaks grudgingly around both sides of them as it meanders slowly toward the Cook Inlet.

When the railroad was being built around 1916, flat-bottomed river boats carried rails and ties upstream as far as Gold Creek. But with its hidden sandbars and tricky currents, the story goes, the river claimed nearly as many rails as did the railroad.

On the west side of the river tall bluffs climb from the bank, keeping their lakes hidden in dense birch forests, sheltering some of Alaska's finest moose and beaver country.

On the east side of the river, the sloping hills roll back full of birch and spruce to deep creases of rivers and streams in the Talkeetna Mountains.

Five miles south of Gold Creek, I waved at some of the Lovell children sledding in their yard. Clyde Lovell and his wife settled there ten years ago, homesteading a piece along the railroad. All their supplies come by train, and Clyde works on Don LaRose's crew to keep the rails smooth and safe along that section of track.

The children are taught by their mother, and Clyde adds rooms to the cabin as the family grows.

Just beyond the Lovell homestead at Sherman, I glanced at my watch and pulled the dogs over to let a freight pass. As always, they asked how I was doing.

As a matter of fact, I was doing better than ever before. Finally, after six days of rough trail, I was able to ride the runners, yell "Hike!" and pretend I was Sergeant Preston happily chasing nasty Jules Laroux, the Yellowknife cat-burglar.

Sending the train along with a wave, I followed it

with that modest string of pound rejects until I rounded a bend and caught it again at Curry, where the crew had stopped for lunch.

Curry used to be a sizable town, but it now is a large section house with a total population of four.

John Lewis, his wife Arnita, and daughter Muriel share the house with a railroad cook, and she, in turn, looks after the freight crews who always stop to eat.

As usual, I was just in time.

While eating my steak, oyster stew, and fresh vegetables, John filled me in on a little of Curry's history. It had, before the fire, boasted a hotel, a school, and homes for the railroad workers. At the base of the hill, the remnants of Alaska's first ski lift could still be seen. In the earlier days, the old steam engines would have to double up to pull the trains "over the hill" to Healy. Curry was the doubling-up spot on the southern end.

Then a fire swept away all but the section house; diesel engines made doubling-up unnecessary, and the bush reclaimed most of Curry for itself.

John and Arnita moved to Alaska from southern Texas nine years before, and consider the move "the best thing we could have done."

John is a savior of the moose along the railroad. He has helped care for starving moose herds along his route in winter, often at his own expense, and endeavors to keep them well away from the tracks.

"When the snow gets deep," John said, "the moose would rather walk along the tracks where the going is easier. The problem is that many moose won't get off the tracks to let the trains go by."

John tries to shoo them off by various means, but is not always successful.

"A moose is a very unpredictable animal," he said, "and is therefore extremely dangerous."

One spring, Lewis came across a cow moose on the tracks at Clyde Lovell's homestead at Sherman. He honked the horn on the gas car, but the moose charged. Quickly, he put the little car in reverse, and backed away until she stopped. Then he ran at her again. This time he threw fusees at her along with honking the horn. All she did was to charge even more determinedly.

This back-and-forth ballet continued for nearly half-an-hour. Neither the moose, nor John, would concede the fight.

Finally the cow charged, and John couldn't get the car into reverse. She reared up, and was about to crash through the front end of the car (which would have killed John instantly) when a shot rang out and the moose dropped dead. Clyde Lovell, who had been watching the drama from his porch, had taken aim with his 30-06, just in case of trouble, and had killed the moose with a clean neck shot.

The hardest moose to move, John said, is a cow with a calf. Unlike many other animals, the calf decides where and when he wants to go, and Mama stays close to see nobody interferes with his decision. Calves will often take a nap on the tracks, and refuse to be disturbed by a gas car, or even a freight. Too often, the best intentions and efforts of the railroad personnel fail to move Junior from his bed, and the train claims another two moose.

Too often, the railroad honchos send out news releases putting the moose kill during the winter (by the trains) at something between twenty and one hundred. The toll is much higher. One year the railroad claimed thirty-nine moose had been taken by the train. John Lewis' records, kept daily, indicated that one-hundred thirty-seven moose had been killed in his seventy-five-mile stretch of track alone. The estimated (unofficially) kill for the entire railroad that winter was close to seven hundred moose.

Just before the tourists come up in June, a special crew works along the tracks, dynamiting moose carcasses out of sight, and taking those they can't blow up into the hollows beneath creek trestles.

Walking the tracks one June, I counted twenty-three dead moose, many pregnant with twins, beneath the trestles in a twelve-mile stretch of track.

The Alaska Railroad has four-hundred seventy miles of track.

Moose are so plentiful along the tracks, in fact, that I had greatly feared at least one major confrontation with one on this trip. Just before leaving Anchorage, I had coffee with two game wardens (but they don't call them that up here) and told them about the trip. Of course, moose are out of season in February, but still I had been warned to take a rifle along.

"You bet," they told me, "take one along, but don't use it unless there is no possible way out. If you kill a moose, clean it, drag it next to the tracks, and tell the railroad people so they can save the meat."

John Lewis thought it a bit unusual that I hadn't run across a moose—and fortunate, too, as often dogs will chase a moose. Catching one would mean the certain end of at least several dogs, perhaps the musher as well.

We talked a bit about it as he helped me with the dogs after that big lunch. With John's help, we got started again. The miles along the peaceful river rolled away until at last we saw ahead the lights of the village of Talkeetna.

Talkeetna was the northern end of the road out of Anchorage and we said goodbye to the railroad tracks. Does that mean the adventure was over? Hardly. No one has ever spent a night in Talkeetna without having an adventure.

100

18

There have been two major events in the history of Talkeetna. The first occurred in 1923 when President Warren G. Harding spent the night in the Fairview Inn before going up to drive the golden spike on the railroad at Nenana.

The second historic event received more notice among the people of the village than the President's visit. It seems that one drunken night, three of the log cabin village's finer citizens calmly stepped out of the bar at the Fairview and punched .30 caliber holes through a trophy moose. His antlers still preside over major drinking functions there in the bar.

The third most historic event in Talkeetna was my arrival there with seven tired dogs. Using the town square as a kennel, I stretched the chain between two trees, snapped the mutts on, and began to head for the Fairview and a little nerve tonic.

But the strange dogs occupying the town square soon had all the local four-footed residents up in arms. Almost immediately the tethered team was surrounded by close to thirty dogs of various sizes and descriptions. Most of them barked at my dogs. Answering threats were made. With all the noise, I expected to be evicted by the town council at any moment. Later, I learned that Talkeetna doesn't have a town council, so I was comparatively safe.

The town didn't pay much attention to the noise, and neither did Big Red. This proud old dog with the ugly face just lay quietly while the rest of the team loudly accompanied his thoughts. One of the town dogs, a large German shepherd, couldn't accept the way Red ignored his teasing and redoubled his efforts. He pranced on his toes with his nose in the air, coming ever closer to the big mongrel. Red didn't care. He walked up to nearly within Red's reach, and lifted his leg. At first, Red tried to ignore it, but when the insults kept streaming, Red had had enough.

With one lunge, Red broke the solid brass snap on the chain. Another lunge took him right into the middle of the stunned German shepherd. The two swung away in a fury of teeth and fur across the park, with Red's teammates howling encouragement

102

from the sidelines, and the town dogs growling for the local champion.

They fought swiftly—so swiftly that I couldn't catch them—then they broke and ran. Red chased the local favorite until he caught him again behind someone's log cabin. It sounded as though two chain saws had come together on the same tree.

The dogs soon disappeared into the woods, followed by yelps, growls and the distinct click of Red's teeth. I didn't expect to see Red again. He had been freed from the pound, had worked hard for two-hundred miles, and now was free even from the work. I walked into the Fairview for some rest.

Talkeetna is beautiful. It is partially decayed, semi-old, bursting with youth, and crusty as hell.

It has the happiest children, the poorest businesses, the oldest condemned buildings, the hardest drinkers, and the longest-winded storytellers in Alaska.

It's like home.

In the bar was Frank Moënnikes, serving drinks and listening to stories. Above his head was the high ceiling, unwashed and stained with forty years' worth of smoke. Animal skins and trophy racks hung on the walls, and a honky-tonk piano sat in the corner beside the juke box.

The rooms are only $5 a night. They are clean, bare, and share a communal bathroom. Frank lends guests some of his paperback westerns to read, and the really hungry can try the refrigerator in the kitchen. They stopped serving regular meals years ago.

Characteristically of Talkeetna and its denizens, no person was ever turned away from the Fairview Inn because he was broke.

After phoning in my stories, I went back to the kitchen to watch myself on the six o'clock news on an ancient set with a six-inch screen. With all the old-timers gathered around, we watched a slide picture of me flash on the screen. Then my pre-taped voice came over the air, telling of the day's activities. It was hard to hear the newscaster's message, however. Each time he said the word "Talkeetna" the boys would cheer.

Frank Moënnikes (pronounced mon-a-kiss) is from Alsace-Lorraine and speaks with a thick German accent. He decided one day that he didn't care enough about Kaiser Wilhelm to fight for him, and came to the United States. How did he get to Talkeetna?

"Vell," said Frank, "von day I vas goink for a ride vis dis friend, und before you know it, ve vas *here!*"

That was forty-nine years ago.

104

Perhaps the best description of Talkeetna ever given came from an interview with Frank by radio reporter Ken Flynn of KHAR in Anchorage:

Flynn: How long have you lived here in Talkeetna, Frank?

Moënnikes: Oh, about forty-nine years now, I guess.

Flynn: Boy! I guess you've seen lots of changes take place in this town during that time!

Moënnikes: No.

Two of the town's favorite characters are Rocky Cummings, age 80, and his partner, Jim Beaver, 62.

The pair has worked the same gold mining ground for over fifty years, and spends the winters in Talkeetna.

Rocky has a sly twinkle and smile, and a sense of humor that could only come from spending fifty years in a hole in the ground.

This time, I did the interviewing.

Me: How large a gold mine do you have, Rocky?

Rocky: Ohhhh, pretty small . . . not so big.

Me: Well, just how big is *that*?

Rocky: We use a Number Two shovel! Heh, heh, heh!

105

Jim Beaver, while not digging in the hole, spends his spare time at the claim planting posies. One time, a bottle of purely medicinal spirits fell from his pocket into the posie bed.

"By God," he said, "fertilizin' pays off, 'cause next spring that bottle began pushing up through the ground and had grown from a fifth into a full quart! We stayed, er . . . ah, *medicated*. . . . for three days!"

Beaver is one of Talkeetna's semi-antiquated official pranksters. He once put colored Easter eggs under one of the neighbor's laying hens.

"After that," he claimed, "every egg she laid had the Northern Lights flashing 'round in the yoke."

I had made my phone call from a booth in the Fairview's lobby. The phone is no longer there. Two months after my visit, both the booth and the phone were destroyed by a sourdough with an ax. From among the coins scattered on the floor, he picked up the two dimes that the operator had "swindled" from him, walked into the next room, and paid Frank the entire cost of the phone.

Falling asleep that night was most difficult. In addition to my worries about locating Red in the morning, the news about the snow conditions farther south were not very promising. The latest reports had bare ground pushing up through the snow a few

106

miles to the south, and no snow at all at Willow, some forty miles distant. The expected snowstorm had failed to appear.

Well, I thought, I'll run it as far as I can, and then give up. No sense in hollering until we're hurt.

There are floor registers in the rooms above the bar, and the laughter and music forced their way up into the room.

The room was bare, but comfortable in an old-fashioned cared-for way. I didn't feel the discomfort that a person usually feels when told that someone had died in this very bed some years before.

Bush pilot Cliff Hudson told me the story:

An old-timer had come to town in the winter, and had run into an old friend of his in the Fairview. Drink followed drink, and in the course of the evening, the old trapper noticed and admired a new suede jacket worn by his friend. The jacket owner said he had just bought it that day, and let his friend wear it.

So the old-timer tried it on, wore it around the bar that evening, and absent-mindedly forgot to take it off. When the night life became a bit too much for him, the old man said goodnight, went upstairs to his bed, and died.

They discovered the body the next morning, and the remains, complete with suede jacket, were taken out to a shed and sealed in a metal case. With the temperature at forty below, there was little danger of spoilage before he could be buried in the spring.

Several days later, the jacket's former owner was drinking in the bar with Hudson and several others, and he was complaining about that new jacket.

"He had a lot of nerve," he said, "dying with that new jacket on. It cost me $40, you know."

"Well why don't you go and get it back?" said Cliff, tired of the griping.

"Well maybe I will!" said the jacket's rightful owner, and he and Cliff went out to the shed.

Cliff talked to him as he unscrewed the many screws holding the lid on the casket.

"Yep," he said, "old Joe would want you to have that jacket. After all, you did pay $40 for it. He won't need it . . . that's for sure."

"That's how I figure," said the other guy, still working at the screws.

"Yeah," Cliff said, "I'll bet old Joe feels real bad about dying in your new jacket. He'd want you to have it too. Of course, we'll have to break both his arms to get it off . . . but hell, old Joe's a good guy, and he wouldn't mind."

"Break his arms?"

"Why, hell yes!" Cliff said. "He's sat out here for three days now at forty below, and he'll be stiffern' a brick. May even have to cut the arms off. . . .

just a little. But old Joe wouldn't mind. After all, you paid $40 for the jacket, and he'd want you to have it."

"Aw hell," said the jacket's owner, putting the screws back in place, "I'll just let Joe have that jacket for a funeral present!"

But even in the same bed where Joe and the now-famous suede jacket had reposed, I began to relax.

Downstairs, Pete Dana was playing the piano, and the customers were singing his composition:

"Oh, we are not all there,
        because we're right here;
Somehow we've all missed the flight;
So here we are in beautiful downtown
        Talkeetna, Alaska tonight!"

"Amen," I smiled, and fell swiftly asleep.

19

Early morning found me making a pretty thorough search of Talkeetna for Big Red. He hadn't returned to the picket chain during the night as I'd hoped, so I combed the village completely.

That took about fifteen minutes.

I hated to just give up the best dog in the team, but there didn't seem to be much choice. Disheartened, I walked up the hill to the sled to get the harnesses.

And there was Red.

He was curled up under the sled, wagging his tail, licking a few wounds, and waiting for me.

Harnessing the dogs wasn't much of a problem that morning, as the cabins in town erupted helpers from all corners. The kids were holding dogs, straightening lines, and having fun. When all was ready, Nameless chewed still another harness, ran to

Cliff Hudson's porch, and returned like a shot with a moose roast in his mouth.   Cliff was in hot pursuit.

The roast sustained only minor damage.

The kids in Talkeetna weren't around for the dog mushing days, and the team was a novelty to them.   The dogs hauled the kids around the park on rides for about half-an-hour before we were ready to start.

From Talkeetna, we would leave the rails that had been our path for so many miles, and mush along the highway.   As we pulled out of town, the fastest runners among the children raced alongside as far as they could, and then yelled goodbye as they dropped back.

Soon we were alone on the icy road.   The going was slick, but we managed nicely until we reached some hills between Talkeetna and Montana Creek.

The road was mostly ice.   It had been packed by four months of heavy equipment and pick-up truck tires, had thawed to water during the occasional chinooks, and had refrozen.   When this mess is inclined at a fairly steep angle, it becomes as difficult to negotiate as walking uphill on a skating rink.

Each trip to the top of a hill was arduous.   Many times I couldn't take my feet off the runners, as I couldn't stand on the surface.   This meant the dogs would have my weight added to that of the loaded sled to pull, and their footing wasn't much better

111

than mine. The sled weighed more then it had in days, as we had picked up fifty pounds of dog food which had been left with Skip Spencer, the stationmaster.

The team's climb up the hill began to resemble a greased pole climbing contest. They would slide back into each other, become tangled, and cry. I couldn't get up to untangle them, either, so they were forced to stay half hobbled until we reached the top.

The schuss down the other side was pure bedlam. Picture seven novice skiers coming down an icy slope too steep for their talents. Connect these imaginary skiers with nylon ropes around their necks and chests, and put a top-heavy sled in the rear. At the rear of the sled, dangle a long-legged ungainly idiot who is scared stiff.

Somehow, with John crying that the sled was running over him, with Shep mysteriously ending up riding down the hill on Randolph's back, and Taffy being jerked down backward, we all made it to the bottom of the hill.

And then, after we had climbed another Matterhorn and skied sideways down the other side, we found . . . Mount Everest.

And so it went for 17 miles, until we had conquered the equivalent of the Alps, the Himalayas, and half of the Catskills.

112

At last the road levelled off, and we continued down the road on fairly smooth going.

Then we began to run out of snow. Small bare patches began to appear in some of the more wind-blown areas. The patches got larger and larger.

We had crossed the Alaska Range, gone through the toughest part of the trip, and were now on the home stretch. The dogs could now make forty miles a day on decent snow, and even the musher was finding new strength in office-slackened muscles. From this area it was a matter of less than one-hundred easy, level miles and we'd be back home in Anchorage.

Between Montana Creek and Sheep Creek, patches of gravel began to pull at the runners, grinding us to a halt. It seemed as though we had come full circle from the snowless roadway at McKinley Park north of the pass.

Striking overland in this area was just as futile as staying on the road. As we descended lower and lower into the Matanuska Valley, the volume of snow in the woods decreased. Now there were only drifts in the shady areas beneath the trees. A few more miles, and there wouldn't be enough to make a sno-cone.

Spring doesn't come until May in this part of Alaska, except for the year 1970, when it came in late February.

Just before the snow gave up entirely, a *Daily News* delivery van pulled up with Stan Abbott at the wheel. After backslapping and talking for some minutes, it became obvious to both of us that this was the end of the trip. We had come over two-hundred miles, and had done rather well, but were cheated out of the final goal. Now, instead of mushing happily and proudly into Anchorage, we would limp in ignominiously in the back of a newspaper delivery truck.

Before we loaded the dogs into the truck, however, Stan asked to drive the team a short ways down the road. He got on the sled, yelled "Hike!" and the boys trotted briskly away. I turned to get in the truck to follow him when I heard some yelling. The lead dogs had looked around, saw Stan on the sled, and saw me back at the truck. They turned around in a wide arc and trotted right back to me.

I was rather embarrassed at their behavior, so we lined them out and tried it again. This time they didn't even get as far as they had the first time, and ran back quickly to the truck.

"Well," said Stan, smiling, "I guess they're your dogs all right!"

We talked a lot on the trip back to Anchorage in the van while the dogs slept in various piles in the back. I learned of the interest that readers had

114

shown in the trip. Some people called the office daily to learn how we were. The dog pound reported about one-hundred fifty more dogs than usual had been "bailed out" of death row. Children had written letters, suggesting names for Nameless. Unfortunately, the paper had erroneously referred to him as a her, so the names were Sugar, Sweetie, Nancy Ann, and Princess. Along with the letters from the kids came invitations to speak at the schools, which I gladly accepted.

We drove to Lloyd Haessler's house in Anchorage, and staked the dogs in the front yard. The following day, I was to drive the dogs down Fourth Avenue during a lull in the Fur Rendezvous dog sled races, for an "official finish."

"Rondy Week" in Anchorage is like Derby Day in Lexington, Kentucky, except that the mania begins one week before the races begin, and lasts for fifty-one weeks after the last dog has gone home. The races themselves take three days, with anywhere from ten to twenty teams running twenty-five miles each day.

People in Anchorage who complain daily about the poodle next door are suddenly quite knowledgeable about George Attla's lead dog; which dog is running the wheel slot for Doc Lombard; and isn't it a shame that old Bowser isn't running for George Hood this year?

115

Bush people come in from villages a thousand miles away to watch their regional champions run the seventy-five miles against the affluent "city" mushers, and the streets are packed with thousands of people from all over the United States, Europe, and Canada.

In the midst of yelling and cheering people and frightened dogs streaming down the hill on Cordova Street (much of the snow had to be hauled in by truck that year) I unloaded the Daily News van, and began harnessing dogs. In almost no time at all, my handler and I were surrounded by youngsters who were eager to help. They could name almost every dog in the team by sight, from the stories I'd written.

In a few minutes, the sled was loaded with the gear, the last racer had sped past, and it was time for us to mush the final six blocks of our run to the finish line in front of Maria's Delicatessen.

After a struggle, the dogs lined out in the center of the street, and started at a trot toward the finish.

My triumphal march was interrupted when the whole team stopped at an intersection. Randolph had taken this opportunity to lift his leg on a policeman who was directing traffic.

We kept weaving down the road, with short time-outs for getting tangled in the crowd and licking the hands of the spectators.

116

About one-hundred yards from the finish line, the dogs perked up and began their quick mushing trot in beautiful pomp and circumstance toward the finish line. Randolph, Taffy, Big Red, Big John, Shep, Jeff, and Nameless in the lead. All of us but Scarface.

We had just crossed the finish line, flash bulbs were popping, and I had reached with my foot for the brake. At that moment, the Rendezvous queen threw a half-nelson on me, dragged me off the back of the sled, and kissed me. It was her job to kiss anything that crossed the finish line.

The dogs went unhindered down the street into the parking lot, and I saw handlers diving for the leaders.

Larry and Kay Fanning were there, and gave me a beautiful model freight sled, and there was also a lantern (the dog mushers' booby prize) with red, white, and blue ribbons on it from the S.P.C.A.

As nice as the radio and television interviews and welcoming was, I had to cut the triumphant entry business short, because the dogs had gone down the road and dived under someone's pickup truck.

20

People who have lived in Anchorage for years can tell you a lot about Alaska, but most of their information is either erroneously picked up in the bar, or read from books.

For some reason, Anchorageites are fairly stationary. Some have been to Fairbanks; a handful have visited Juneau; a bunch have gone down to Seward (one-hundred twenty-seven miles south) for the Salmon Derby. Almost none have been to the villages or the bush.

Anchorage (population almost 50,000) is nevertheless a big city with the same functions as Los Angeles, St. Louis, or Chicago. It is a city. It will always be a city, and only in a few places where trappers and villagers meet can any bush flavor be found.

As one friend put it, "Anchorage is the closest city to Alaska."

Anchorage has Alaska's first freeway. It's known

as the Spenard Thru-way, the Minnesota By-pass, or "That new Spenard Road thing," depending on whether you're a resident, a highway engineer, or an old-time Alaskan.

It is, nevertheless, Alaska's longest freeway, stretching just over a mile between Anchorage and Spenard (which abut each other).

The state's other freeway is a half-mile of blacktop which stretches from one end of Juneau to the other.

Anchorage does have traffic problems, however, and with traffic snarls come radio planes. Anchorage's radio reporters broadcast during "rush hour", which lasts for fifteen minutes twice daily.

The broadcasts sound something like this:

"Well folks, here we are high above the downtown section of Anchorage to report on the traffic conditions this foggy afternoon. I think we're approaching . . . yes, we are . . . we are coming up on Northern Lights Boulevard now. . . . In fact, we're almost directly above it now, and can spot the traffic conditions for you listeners on this foggy afternoon here in the city of Anchorage.

"Yes, it's getting plainer now, and the cars are coming in sight. In fact, there is some traffic activity plainly visible below us . . . wouldn't you say, Joe?"

Joe is the pilot who gives free plane rides each day in return for plugs on the air.

"Yes, Joe, I think we can safely say that traffic is moving normally on Northern Lights Boulevard as we cruise smoothly overhead in this beautiful Cessna 172 owned by Joe's Flying Service at Merrill Field. Just how long the normal traffic conditions on this thoroughfare remain is hard to say, but we'll check on it later to let you listeners know just how it is going on this foggy afternoon . . . Now, isn't that Fifth Avenue appearing under our sleek left wing as our Cessna 172 smoothly banks around over downtown Anchorage? Yes, I believe it is, and in just a minute, we'll tell you listeners how the traffic is holding out on that popular thoroughfare . . ."

The effectiveness of this traffic report is phenomenal. Inside twenty minutes, everyone in Anchorage has miraculously found his way home.

Not only is Anchorage first in the state with traffic reports, but it is also quickly going to the fore in urban planning. After lengthy meetings, the city fathers decided that in order for Anchorage to take its rightful place among large cities, it needed ghettoes.

Ghettoes were rather hard to come by at first. In the early days, short-sighted residents lived in cabins or tents here and there without any regard for race, religion, or social standing. Over the years, however, and with diligent efforts on the parts of city planners, this deplorable condition began to change.

120

Snarling in the face of antiquated Alaskan tradition, the working class began thoughtfully to stick together in the suburb of Spenard.

The rich people, not to be left behind socially, moved to Turnagain until 1964. In that year, an earthquake of some magnitude helped Turnagain become part of the Pacific Ocean, and the rich people moved a little farther back from the coastline.

The poorer people took up residence near the downtown area, mostly, in the older housing.

The southerners moved to Mountain View and Muldoon, which are now famous as the "Laundromat Capital of Alaska."

The smart people moved to the bush, and were never heard from again.

In all, Anchorage had become a metropolis. It is possible in the course of an afternoon to have coffee at the Westward and talk to political hacks, public relations men, and other unscrupulous types, walk two blocks to Maria's Delicatessen and keep up with the new generation, go three doors and have a beer with Natives from the villages, and drive across town and be bored to death at the golf course.

Unfortunately, Anchorage is still cursed with a magnificent view of five different mountain ranges. The chamber of commerce has been working diligently on this problem. They have decided to make people pay for the view. By an ingenious program, they encouraged people to build skyscrapers, putting a bar on the top floor of each one. Whereas previously the view was available to everyone, now the buildings compete in height to sell beers to view lovers. The more beers sold, the more money comes to the coffers of Anchorage, and progress marches on.

One new building in the downtown area outdid all others. Its seven floors on the entire south side of the building have one-way mirror windows. This was a stroke of pure genius. The sun, reflecting off the mirrored floors, blinded late afternoon motorists, and helped stimulate the economy through the tow truck and new-car-sales businesses.

As if that weren't a large enough boon to mankind, the windows are directly across the street from a section of park used by youngsters in the winter as a skating rink. The reflected heat made skating more comfortable by transforming the rink into a wading pool.

There is now a rumor that the poorer areas will be stimulated by construction of unheated tenement buildings, but that is almost too much to hope for.

21

As attractive as life in Anchorage has become, a dog musher soon becomes addicted to the sport. But open country is needed, so I shortly found myself looking into the possibilities of a second sled trip.

The summer presented fairly rough sledding (no snow). I kept busy doing other stories in the meantime. While on assignment for the paper, I lived in two Tlingit Indian villages in southeastern Alaska; rode on board a research vessel studying poisonous clams; interviewed every topless dancer in Anchorage (not a bad assignment), and took one of the young ladies with me on a canoe trip down the Yukon River. And we'd have done it, too, but the car fell apart near a ghost town named Chicken, and we had to call it off. Then followed a week's visit to

Adak Island in the Aleutians for the annual Oklahoma Days celebration; the installation of several bush libraries (our readers supplied the books); a trip to the North Slope oil fields, and a week spent at the Jesse Lee Home for children.

These last two stuck in my mind particularly, and the next sled trip was a direct consequence of both these visits.

The Jesse Lee Home can handle about forty-five children at any time. The home has been famous as an orphanage in Alaska since pioneer days, but now it specializes in kids with serious emotional problems. The children are of all ages and races and come from all parts of the state. I developed a real liking for the home and the children during my visits there. My job was to "hang around," sopping up atmosphere and facts for a series of stories on the place.

As good a job as the home does for children, however, it is the only facility of its type in the state, and there are an estimated 13,000 children in Alaska in need of this service.

The home's director, Dick Gilbert, had mentioned the need for a paved play yard for the kids, which could be used as a hockey rink in winter, a basketball court in summer, and for fun the rest of the year.

More and more I thought of raising the necessary

124

money for the yard. Then a gong crashed in my head. Why not make a dog sled trip to raise the money? And why not on the North Slope, with all that open country?

The North Slope oil fields, the pipeline they intended to build, and the route the pipe was to take were very much in the news at that time. Why couldn't I go to the North Slope with a dog team, pick up a quart of oil, and mush south the 800 miles with it to the port at Valdez (pronounced val-deez).

I rushed in to Larry Fanning's office with the great plan.

"Hey Larry, how about letting me mush a quart of oil down from the North Slope to Valdez? I'd only be gone a month or so."

"You're crazy!" he said, mumbling some question about the propriety of my immediate ancestry.

Of course, I couldn't really expect to win him over very easily, but I kept between him and the door for several hours. When it looked as though he would miss lunch, and possibly dinner, he gave in.

"Okay," he said, "give it a try. But the newspaper can't afford anything more than your time on this trip, so you'll have to promote the money somehow."

"Right!" I said, not knowing how to promote more than a cup of coffee in Anchorage.

"And it had better be a safe trip," he added, "we want you back in one piece."

"No sweat!"

No sweat? It was about that time I began to wonder just how good an idea this was. I had done my homework first, of course, and knew the route well. Well, I knew the route fairly well. Well, actually a good portion of it lay through uncharted country in the Brooks Range, and nobody knew it well, so it was easy to learn as much about it as anybody else knew.

The Alyeska Pipeline Company was the logical place to go for advice and help. They were the ones who had to build a pipeline through that country.

I began my "tin cupping" (as Fanning called it) the following day.

At Alyeska, Buddy Morrell was quite helpful. He told me I was crazy. Then he told me I shouldn't try it. Then he told me to look at some photographs of the country first.

The stack of aerial photos showed a bleak snow-covered rockpile, with various arrows marked on it.

"That's the Brooks Range," he said, pointing. "The pipe will go through this pass."

The Dietrich Pass has terrible winds, he said, deep snow, and it gets very cold there in the winter. The company maintained pipeline camps along

126

the route, but some were fifty miles apart.   If anything happened, and a storm came up, the rescuers quite likely couldn't get to me in less than three or four days, depending on the length of the storm.

Then he said the company couldn't sponsor the trip, but would give me a meal and a bed *if* I got as far as one of their camps.

Then he looked at me smugly and asked if I still planned to go.

"Sure," I said.

"Well," he said, "I'd better talk this over with the brass."

Several days passed before I saw Buddy again, and when I did, he seemed a bit more optimistic about the trip, but just a bit.

He took me to meet David Henderson, who was an even bigger honcho with the outfit.   Henderson, who speaks with a British accent (I suspect he came from the British Petroleum part of the oil conglomerate) wished me well on the venture, and asked Morrell if they (Alyeska) couldn't help out a little.   Morrell said he wasn't sure.

After several weeks of planning, the "go date" in November kept creeping closer, and I had only managed to borrow a healthy twelve-foot freight sled, and a few dog harnesses.

A November start seemed sound at the time.   In November, I would have sufficient snow cover on the Slope for mushing, and I would be crossing the Arctic Circle (I hoped) before the full three months of darkness fell. By following winter south, I could cross the Yukon when it was hard and safe, and be off the trail by January, when Alaska's really cold weather strikes.

Had I talked to an Eskimo on the Slope before going, my starting date would have been early March, but Barrow Eskimos are hard to find in Anchorage.

A few days later, and barely a week before I was to start, things began to click in my direction. People I had never heard of came to my aid. Area Realtors chipped in $125 for my food; Maria's Delicatessen donated $100 for equipment; Stewart's Photo Shop loaned me a 35mm camera; Wien Consolidated Airlines offered to fly team and musher to Prudhoe Bay; the Ralston Purina Company donated enough dog food to keep my eleven dogs well-fed through the trip; and the dog pound donated eleven dogs.

And then, Alyeska Pipeline called me in.

"We can't sponsor you, officially," Morrell said, "but we could help a little maybe to see that you're safe."

When the interview was over, I walked away stunned.

Alyeska Pipeline had not only promised hospitality in the camps along the way, but had offered to fly daily air cover for me in helicopters, and loaned me a walkie-talkie, a flashing strobe light, a heavy down sleeping bag, and $173 to purchase some snowshoes and other equipment I needed.

All that remained was to get some heavy Arctic clothing for the trip. Through a friend, the Alaska Air National Guard outfitted me completely—from parka to mukluks. Their clothes had never been field tested for more than an hour or two in extreme weather, and they were anxious for a report.

In just a few days' time, I was ready for the trip. I had run the dogs a few times in the shallow snow around my cabin at Indian, and picked eleven good ones for the trip.

Then I ran into Stan Barney.

If you have ever run across the old-fashioned horse trader, you will have little trouble recognizing Stan Barney. But Stan Barney is a dog musher. His teams rank well each year, even in some of the biggest races in the world, but his real fun comes in talking dogs with other mushers.

I had gone into a place where liquid refreshment mingled with games of pocket billiards to celebrate how well the trip was shaping up, and met Stan, who was busy adding to the gross national product of Tumwater, Washington.

I told him about the trip.

"What are you running up front?" (the lead position) he asked.

"Oh, just some of last year's dogs."

"My God! Don't you know you'll get killed doing that? Oh, Slim, you can get along fine with those pound bummers along the railroad tracks, of course, 'cause them dogs just trot along ever so nicely between the rails. But man, you can't go to the Slope with pound bummers in the lead! There's wide open spaces up there with no trails at all. No roads, no nothin'. You just gotta have a front end on that team!"

"Well," I said, "what do you suggest?"

"Well now, I just got a little dog the other day, by golly," he said, putting his arm around my shoulders and steering me toward another beer, "that would do you just right up there. He's a perfect lead dog from a team I bought out of Unalakleet, and he's a beauty. I wouldn't take $5,000 for that dog. . . . I mean it . . . he's priceless . . . but I'll let you take him along on this trip to give him a few miles before the racing season starts."

"No way," I told him. "Last year I lost one dog in a fight. I'll be darned if I'll take someone else's top lead dog to the slope and have him get killed one way or the other. I'll just make do with what I have."

130

"Never mind that," Stan said, waving away my argument. "If he gets killed . . . well, that's the breaks, and just shove him in a hole someplace. If he doesn't work out for you, just knock him in the head, but if he does all right for you, just bring him on home with you, as I'll want him for this season."

"Are you sure, Stan?"

"Slim," he said, clutching his heart, "if anything happened to you on the Slope because you didn't have a good front end on that team, why, I don't know what I'd do. Now you just take old Prince on up there and then I'll be able to sleep at night, knowing that you're in good hands."

And that's how I came to get Prince.

He even had a regal-sounding name! What a windfall! Now I could just stand back on the sled with one of those fabled lead dogs that were so nice to run up there on the front end, and my worries were over!

In my excitement at being offered this dog, I overlooked the fact that Barney's offering me a $5,000 lead dog "to see if he works out all right," was the unlikely equivalent to Howard Hughes loaning me a Cadillac and telling me that if the ride weren't smooth enough, I should feel free to drive it over a cliff.

But other things kept me busy at home and at the

office, and I didn't meet Prince until two hours before plane time in mid-November.

I needed a handler to help me the first few days on the slope while we would be getting the team ready and sorting out who-goes-where in the starting line-up. The perfect handler showed up in the person of Dave Jones, my neighbor, and an avid dog fan. Dave and I had lived in the small farming town of Oakdale, California, at the same time, but hadn't met until we were both in Alaska. Dave had developed an interest in the dogs, and, as he was temporarily unemployed, said he'd love to come along.

No better man could've been found.

Tragedy struck the kennels at home several days before I left. Big Red, my last dog from the earlier trip, had an enemy in camp named Mike. Mike was a beautiful Malemute, weighing 110 pounds, and could pull a sled like sixty, but he hated Red.

One day while I was gone, Mike broke his collar and tore into Red, who was still chained up. By the time I arrived home, Red had bled to death. With tears for an old friend, I buried him beneath the soil of the Turnagain Arm under a full moon.

With the loss of Red, and the addition of Prince, I still had eleven dogs, and soon the time came to leave. The plane left Anchorage for Prudhoe Bay

132

at six a.m., which meant that we had to have the dogs loaded in the plane by four a.m.

After all the loading and packing had been done, we set off for the airport, twenty-five miles away, with a stop first at Stan Barney's to pick up Prince.

Naturally, we had to have a beer at Stan's before talking dogs. . . . and then another one. Stan waxed brilliant over the dog's prowess, and I was fairly gloating with happiness and good fortune. At last he told me to wait a minute, and he'd bring in the dog.

Wondering what this great leader looked like, I paced the living room. Suddenly, there was a burst of cussing musher and howling dog. The back door crashed open, and in poured a gyrating combination of man and dog. The dog managed to break free of Stan's hold, and annihilated the kitchen table on his way into the living room. A number of beer cans fell in the onslaught, and Stan slipped in the foamy suds while diving for the dog. He executed a neat half-gainer with a French twist, and slid into the bookcase.

Prince, by this time heard Nature's call, and answered in the midst of a ricochet between the sofa and the television set. Finally cornered against the wall, he trembled and shook.

Stan grabbed the good-looking black-and-white

sled dog, called him something other than Prince, and turned to me with beer streaming down his clothes and a smile on his face.

"You see how alert he is?" Stan said. "He's about the best sonofabitch I ever had!"

It took three men to load him into the truck, and we drove to the airport.

22

The medium-range jet airliner sat with its auxiliary engine whining, and the huge cargo doors open. After several minutes of paperwork, Dave and I handed the dogs up to the men in the plane, one by one.

They were placed in a four-by-eight-foot pen designed to carry sled dogs from the villages in to the races. Each dog was snapped up short to the side of the pen. It was good arrangement. No dog could move enough to start a fight, unless some stupid neighbor stuck his tail in another's mouth. Miraculously, all eleven dogs fit snugly into the pen. It was covered with a sheet of plywood, and the heavy sled and gear placed on top. The dogs wouldn't be bothering the stewardesses on the flight anyway.

Dave and I, worn by a sleepless night, drove to the main terminal for some coffee and breakfast. We were shortly joined by Henry Peck, the quiet photographer of the *Daily News*, who was to go with us for the first day or two.

After the first cup of coffee, we learned of the plot to hitchhike on the plane with us. Three reporters from the *News* came bounding into the coffee shop after having celebrated freely all night. The trio was led by Allan Frank, wearing my favorite Stetson. I noticed my moccasins on his feet, too. Following in polite staggers close behind were Barry Flynn, sportswriter, and Will Lawson, political analyst and later press secretary to the governor.

They grinned sheepishly.

"What the . . . . ?"

"Now, Slim, just relax," Allan said. "We're going with you. We went out to your cabin, but missed you there . . ."

"That's my hat and moccasins . . ."

"Thought they'd give us some class. . . . so I borrowed 'em," he said, "but we're going with you to do the great story of the North Slope Oil Race! Exciting, isn't it? Wow! Old Amundsen and Peary've got nothing on the good old *Daily News*. Now we're going to come aboard the plane on the pretense of interviewing you, and then hide somewhere while the stewardess isn't looking. . . . see? . . . then, after the plane takes off . . ."

"Look," I said, knowing that these bozos were entirely capable of such antics, "if you guys mess up this free plane ride for me, I'll kill all three of you!"

"Aw, now Slim . . ."

"I mean it, dammit. . . . I worked too hard for this, and you just butt out!"

Allan didn't look the least bit in a butting-out attitude, and Lawson and Flynn just grinned.

We all had coffee together until the plane was called, and then Dave, Henry and I walked to the plane, keeping a close eye over our shoulders for the Mad Musketeers. They were standing behind the big glass doors, waving handkerchiefs and feigning parting sobs.

I was more than relieved when we checked the dogs, informed the stewardesses of their presence, and took seats in the front row in case we had to go forward to handle them.

Then we leaned back in the seat for some well-earned rest.

I caught the waving motion in the corner of my eye just before it closed. Outside, and running toward the plane were three figures, waving notebooks and shouting "Stop the press!"

Allan Frank, as always in the lead, had stuck a press card in the band of my cowboy hat. I groaned audibly and sank down in the seat. It did no good. The stewardess found me.

"Sir," she said, sweetly, "there are some gentlemen from the press outside who say they must see you. They said it's important. I don't know what to do."

"Tell them I have no further statements on the price of barley, and that the baby isn't due until March."

We saw no more of the jet pirates, and the plane taxied out and gunned off into the winter sky without further incident.

The silence of the smooth ride to Fairbanks (where we refueled), was broken only by Henry, who sat clicking away at my face with his 35mm picture box as we flew.

"It's a shame," he said.

"What's a shame?" I asked.

"Well," he said, "the light in here isn't too good. You see, I have to shoot at 2.8 at a sixtieth. Of course, that brings down my depth-of-field to almost nothing, and I have to decide whether it's best to get your eyes in focus or your nose."

"Eyes," I said, sleepily. "Nothing spectacular about the nose. Broken twice."

"That just gives it character," he said, zeroing in on my nose, "but if I just had a couple more stops of light, I could get your hairline, and your Adam's apple . . ."

138

"Forget the Adam's apple, Henry . . ."

"If we could just get a little more light on your face. Now outside it's plenty light enough . . ."

"We're at thirty thousand feet, Henry, and I don't feel like sitting on the wing."

"You must be tired," he said.

I'm still trying to figure that one out.

After dozing on the plane, and dozing some more in the Fairbanks terminal, we were back in the air, headed due north over some of the roughest country in the world. Perhaps it was a blessing I couldn't see the Brooks Range on that snowy day, or I might have decided to ride back home on the plane.

We began our descent through thick clouds, the little chime dinged, followed by the captain (who, incidentally, is Eskimo) telling us we were about to land at the Deadhorse Airport, seven miles south of Prudhoe Bay.

We dropped lower, and the clouds got thicker. We heard the whirring of the flaps being lowered, but could no longer see them. Then the gear chunked into place, still with no visibility, and I began to wonder if we were being talked down by one of the F.A.A. boys.

Then we broke through the clouds, and could see the tiny square camps of Deadhorse about two-hundred feet beneath the plane. Everything was white—desolately and completely white—and flat. The bright orange of some of the buildings

139

showing where the wind-driven snow hadn't curved over it completely. Down there was immense wealth, and immense cold, and unearthly desolation. Down there was adventure.

The plane touched down and rolled to a stop.

It was exactly zero degrees as we unloaded the dogs, staked them out, and went into the hangar for coffee. The room was filled with men dressed in Arctic gear. They were representatives of the far-flung oil camps, and had driven over for the mail.

Alyeska's Crazyhorse Camp was but a mile away, and had sent two men to help us move our dogs and gear.

After coffee, we bundled against the cold, and went out to move the outfit to camp. After much struggling, the dogs were loaded into the back of the pick-up, but we still had a heavy, well-loaded freight sled to move. Dave simply tied the sled to the trailer hitch on the truck. I stepped on the runners, and was pulled to camp behind several hundred horses.

In the camp yard were many pieces of heavy equipment that would not be used until the Interior Department gave the go-ahead for the building of the pipeline. We strung the long heavy picket chains between the bumpers of two of these, and chained each dog.

Then we went in for lunch.

140

Crazyhorse Camp was just like the other camps along the shores of the Beaufort Sea. It consisted of many modular units linked together into rooms, hallways, showers, kitchen and dining rooms. Each unit had been built in Seattle, floated on a barge over 5,000 miles to Prudhoe Bay during the brief summer, and dragged to its site. The camps looked like modern mobile homes, with a few exceptions.

Each building is raised three or more feet off the ground, so that most of the hurricane-blown snow can pass beneath the building rather than over the top. This doesn't always work.

For another, each had about one foot of insulation between the imitation panelling on the inside wall, and the aluminum siding on the outside. The most obvious differences, however, were the doors. Each outside door was thick and heavy, and had a heavy metal pull handle exactly like those used in butchers' walk-in freezers. This was to keep the cold *out*, however, and the heat *in*.

Outside sat the company pick-ups, resembling horses tied to the hitch rail. Each was connected to the rail by an electrical cord that activated the truck's head bolt and gas tank heaters. During periods of extreme cold, the practice is to start the truck's engine and let it run for awhile before unplugging the heaters. Many trucks have been frozen in the time it takes to unplug the heater, jump in the cab, and start the truck. When parked where no plug is available, the trucks are always left running.

If all this makes it sound like pretty cold country—it is.

Inside the buildings, however, all was cheery, warm, and bright. We were shown to our room, which had two bunks in it, separate reading lamps, and an ample closet. Most Arctic gear was left in the hallway on the false porch (between the inner and outer doors of the buildings).

The dining-living area of the camp was designed to provide men with all the leisure-time activities it could. The companies do not allow booze, women, or guns on the North Slope—with good reason—so they try to compensate in other ways.

At the end of the room was a pull-down movie screen. Movies are shown almost nightly in every camp, and often the men will get on the radio, learn what's playing at the other camps, and drive over to see that show. There is also a much-used pool table, and a ping-pong table. Tony, the Austrian-born cook at our camp, was the acknowledged champ of the North Slope ping-pong fraternity.

One of the men owned a tape deck, which played Buck Owens and Merle Haggard many hours during the day, and the food . . . the food . . . the food!

142

Men burn up a lot of calories working in extreme cold, but the men on the Slope usually return quite a bit fatter to their families. The reason for this is the most extravagant horn of plenty I have ever witnessed. Had I stayed two more days, a name change would have been in order.

Besides the three meals each day (all you can eat of steaks, fried chicken, and all the trimmings, etc.) there is a constant supply of readily consumable food sitting on tables in the dining room. Since the crews work round-the-clock shifts, there must always be something for them to eat at three a.m. or whenever.

When a crew comes in, tired, cold, and hungry in the middle of the night, they go to the large warming oven, taking out the complete evening meals which were left there for them by the cook earlier in the evening. If they manage to get through all that food (which is unlikely) and are still hungry (which is even more unlikely) they can avail themselves of the "snack table." On this table lie bowls of fresh fruit, cookies, cake, at least two pies, chocolate eclairs, and cold sandwiches. Crossing the room to the drink dispensers, they have their choice of coffee, milk, hot tea, iced tea, hot chocolate, and Kool-Aid.

They can then take a hot shower of limitless length and crawl between the fresh clean sheets the bull-cooks have provided that day.

All this is in addition to wages that sometimes (but not always) average $1,500 per week. So the next time a Texan gives a hard-luck story about the rigors of life on the Arctic Slope, tell him to go kick an icicle.

It was plain that the oil rush of the 'seventies would be conducted much differently than the gold rush of the turn of the century. Had the men in the Klondike had the accommodations afforded the Prudhoe Bay roughnecks, there would still be plenty of gold in the Yukon. Nobody would have left camp to go look for it.

After a filling lunch, Dave and Henry and I went out to take the dogs on a trial spin around the area. We harnessed the dogs, putting Prince in the lone lead spot, and once again I yelled "Hike!"

Prince shot off down the road, and the rest of the team got tangled. After we unstrung the mess, we tried it again, this time with better results. We slid effortlessly down the road, with Dave jogging along behind, and Henry backing up out in front, snapping pictures. Then we hit a bare spot, and the sled ground to a halt on the gravel.

The roads at Prudhoe Bay are masterpieces of engineering. They are all built on fill, raising the roadway about five vertical feet above the swampy level of the tundra. In winter, the winds keep the snow blown clear of the road, and the roads never

144

have to be plowed. This is excellent for machinery, but it plays hell with a man's dog mushing.

The snow piles up on each side of the road, however, meaning that if you should step or drive off onto the shoulder, you sink into a five-foot drift.

After about a mile of pretty frustrating mushing, we pulled off the road and followed some heavy equipment tracks we'd found cutting overland. This worked fine—except for Prince.

This magnificent $5,000 lead dog, this pillar of Unalakleet's canine community, refused to follow a trail.

He would be running along just right, and would then plunge off into soft snow, floundering pitifully in the mess. I could yell "Gee!" or "Haw!" until the cows came home, and he would look at me as though I were crazy.

It would then be necessary to walk past all ten of the other dogs, grab him, and set him back onto the trail. He would start out and do just fine for about another hundred yards, then back into the snow he would go, with a pitiful smirk on his face.

Dave and I talked it over and decided that, since he came from a Bering Sea village, perhaps he spoke only Inupiat Eskimo. I had come to know many Eskimo mushers, and they all used "Gee" and "Haw" for directional commands—except—except for the people who live on St. Lawrence Island.

For some reason known only to them, the people of that island's two villages, Gambell and Savoonga, use "Put" and "Stubbit" for their commands. (Folk history blames the early whalers, who said "Port" and "Starboard", for this departure from mushing regulations.) I tried "Put" and "Stubbit" on Prince, just in case he had once been across the sea to Gambell, but with the same negative results. Worse, all the dogs in the team looked back at me as though I had finally taken complete leave of my senses. It was too much to bear.

"Hell," said Dave, his face mask frosty white with ice, "old Wolf knows how to follow the path of least resistance."

So Wolf and his teammate, Ralph, were put into the lead, and Prince was relieved of command and placed in the swing position behind them. This system worked well. At first, Prince continued his snowy dives, but this time Wolf and Ralph would pull together and drag him back onto firmer snow. After a mile or so, Prince gave up, and just pulled his share behind the leaders.

After several hours of shakedown running, we returned to camp, quite satisfied with the team, and with its chances of making the long haul eight-hundred miles to Valdez.

We staked the dogs, fed them, and took a nap before dinner.

During dinner that evening (it got dark at two-thirty p.m.) we learned that one camp about fifteen miles away needed a truck driver. Dave, an unemployed truck driver, wanted to look into the situation. We borrowed a pick-up and drove over to the camp, getting lost only twice on the way.

The camp was much the same as the one we had just left, but a little larger. While Dave was talking to the foreman about the job, I sat in on a game of eight-ball which had drawn an unusual number of spectators from the ranks of the off-duty men.

Neither man was a pool shark, and any commercial fisherman could have beaten them both at the game. But when at last the eight-ball sank on a two-cushion shot, there was applause from the spectators, and the winner and loser walked off together to another room.

Asking one of the men why there was so much interest taken in the game, he explained that it was the culmination of a week's arguing between the men, and each one of the players had put $400 on the outcome!

To make an unusual evening even more interesting, Dave got the job.

23

Dave and I both awoke before dawn the following day. It isn't hard to do. The sun doesn't rise until ten a.m.

After breakfast, we visited with the men, learning some of the jobs they had. Most of the men were core drillers for Alyeska Pipeline. Their job was to travel the pipeline route, drilling test holes every so often. These samples of dirt were then sent to laboratories to be analyzed as to how much weight they could bear. These tests were necessary to the construction of a safe pipeline.

Some of the other men, like Buck and Smokey, were old hands in the oil field business, and had been sent by their respective companies to report on the trials and tribulations of pumping oil across land that froze into near-concrete half the year, and thawed to the consistency of oatmeal mush the other half. The two of them had been friends for years, and their humor helped to brighten things when an Arctic storm would seal off the camp.

Dave and I mended harnesses and repaired rigging for the rest of the pre-dawn hours. One dog in particular, Wolf, was especially hard on harness. He had the habit of turning around, chewing through the backstraps, and running free down the trail. This was a poor idea for two reasons. The main reason was that Wolf was supposed to be the lead dog, and where his whims and fancies took him, he was followed by ten others. This disagreeable habit of his had taken us beneath a building one time, and through a pile of frozen heavy equipment another time.

The other reason was that dog harnesses cost five bucks apiece.

Wolf's taste in teething equipment wasn't cured until much later in the year when I was struck with a brilliant idea. One night, I soaked the backstraps of his harness in a mixture of water and tabasco sauce. The next day, he chewed through the last harness he would ever consider biting. This action took place in front of a large group of people, and they thought I had an acrobatic dog. One man offered me a dollar if I'd get him to do it again, but Wolf wasn't in the mood for instant replays.

When the darkness began to lift from the snowy

149

flats, Dave and I harnessed the team, driving them seven miles to the Atlantic-Richfield (Arco) "Hilton" at Prudhoe Bay. We had left one dog back in camp, however. Mike, the big Malemute that I counted on to break the sled free of ice each day, was looking very sick. He hadn't touched the food we'd given him the night before, and appeared to be running a fever. His normal enthusiastic bounce had declined to a slight wag of that great tail.

We had decided to see if he would improve during our absence.

That day's mushing was so much better than the previous day's, that our spirits lifted considerably. The ten dogs had become a team of sorts. Prince had stopped dodging off into snowbanks, and Wolf failed to destroy a single backstrap all day.

At the Arco Hilton, a lavish $3-million hotel that houses over one-hundred men, we met with officials and were given several quarts of oil to take to Valdez. The oil came from the Put River Number One well, the confirmation well that decided the oilmen on paying over $900 million to lease the drilling rights from the state.

Starting back, Wolf decided he would take a shortcut back to camp. Before we could dissuade him, he had cut across the road and straight across the hard-packed runway of the Prudhoe Bay airstrip.

Now when ten dogs decide to go a certain direction, and all the musher has is a brake that's ineffectual on hard-packed snow, he either hangs on and goes along—or is left behind.

When we reached the other side, Wolf then decided to go into the F.A.A. tower for coffee. This slowed him down enough that Dave and I could run up and grab him. We tied the team outside and went in to apologize.

The controllers were laughing when we arrived, and pointed out the window. Through the grey-black of evening, a Hercules aircraft touched down and reversed his engines, throwing huge sprays of snow in the air.

"That poor pilot thinks we're crazy," one of them laughed. "We saw you coming, and told him he'd have to hold for a minute, because we had a dog team on final approach!"

Pretty soon the pilot came in, looking the dogs over carefully on his way.

"I thought you guys were getting 'bushy'," he said, "but I owe you an apology. I'm the one that's going nuts."

We explained the trip to him, then, and we all had coffee.

When we left, we drove the dogs home at a good clip, under a full moon—at three o'clock in the afternoon.

151

With a sled that was nearly empty (except for Dave's weight), we sailed along. This would have been fine, except that the temperature was minus eighteen degrees, and our speed against the slight breeze put the chill factor to nearly fifty below.

When we pulled into camp, both of us were thoroughly cold. Our faces were heavy masks of ice over the knitted hoods we wore beneath our parkas. Wearing glasses, I was nearly blind from the frost coating on the lenses. This was a daily problem for me in the Arctic. My breath would come up through the face mask, and emerge through the slot left open for the eyes. It would then strike the icy glass and freeze solid.

I asked several of the men up there who wore glasses about a possible solution, but they knew of none.

Mike hadn't improved a bit during the day, so we took him in to the false porch, which was kept at about fifteen degrees above zero. When he turned up his nose at some raw steak the cook took out to him, I knew we had a very sick dog.

After dinner we again borrowed a pick-up, and drove the seven miles to the Arco Hilton, hoping to find the North Slope's only physician.

Dr. Felt, who has a regular practice in Fairbanks, was upstairs watching the daily film when we arrived. When the film ended, I asked him if he would mind taking a look at the dog. He was not a veterinarian, of course, but agreed immediately, and had us take the dog to one of the heated garages, where he met us.

He checked the dog carefully for several minutes, but then shook his head.

"Darned if I know what's wrong with him," he said, "but he seems to be running a fever, and his eyes don't look so good. I can give him a penicillin shot if you like. It might help, if it's an infection of some kind, and I don't think it will hurt him any."

The doc gave him a shot. Thankfully, he held still for it. Almost immediately, Mike got up and walked over to a faucet and began to lick it. We located a hard hat and filled it with water for him. He drank four hard hats full of water before we left.

Back in camp, Mike drank water for about an hour, then lay down to rest. Three hours later, he was ravenously hungry, and ate two steaks and about three pounds of dog food. The next morning, he jumped all over us, and I knew he was on the road back.

24

Leaving Mike in camp again that day to recuperate, I decided to test the team with a loaded sled. We had said goodbye to Dave that morning, as he had left for his new job.

The dogs found a cat trail running through the tundra, and followed it quickly to Prudhoe Bay. Even with five-hundred pounds on the sled, the dogs took the first mile or so in a lope. We made it to the "Hilton" an hour ahead of my estimate.

Going inside to have coffee, I sat with several of the men in the main lobby, listening to their stories. They all agreed that the most fascinating part of life at Prudhoe Bay was the crossings they sometimes made on the ice pack, about one-half mile north of the camp.

154

With the rest of the day to kill, I thought I'd drive the dogs out and see what it was like.

I've never been sorry that I did.

We drove along the road in temperatures about minus twenty, passed the "pipe yard" with its hundreds of miles of forty-eight-inch pipe, and arrived at the dock. One lone barge was frozen fast in the ice. The early pressure of the ice as it is formed each year pushes great masses of it into the air. One such pressure ridge extended from the end of the dock, so I drove the dogs right off the end of the dock and onto the pack ice.

For several thousand miles ahead of me, the ice stretched unbroken to Norway and Greenland. The pack, with its fissures and pressure ridges, engraves a scene on the memory which is never erased.

The dogs had good firm footing, and the ice slipped by noiselessly and quickly beneath the steel on the runners. We glided along on the ice pack for nearly an hour, nearing several islands about seven miles offshore. Then we turned around and rested before starting the return trip.

One of the reasons for these shakedown trips was to try and arrange the team of dogs in the most efficient order. Having much more experience than when making the first trip, I planned to use these days of acclimation to put together the best team I could, and avoid the heartbreak that comes with putting the wrong dog in the lead. There, on the Beaufort Sea, I discovered Tanya.

Tanya had belonged to a family of apartment-dwellers in Anchorage. When she outgrew the apartment, the family tried to find a home for her. In desperation, they called the pound for help. I was called, took one look at the dog, and we have been together ever since.

Tanya is a big (85 pounds) silver grey cross between a Malemute and a Siberian. For the first few days, I had run her in the wheel position next to Mike.

However, I noticed not only the almost religious frenzy that she threw into her work, but also other little things. She would raise her head and look around as the team would approach some animals, such as the fat white ptarmigan, when the others didn't seem to be aware of their presence.

By now I knew what qualities to look for in a leader, and this quiet grey female begged for an audition.

I put her up front next to Wolf, and slipped Ralph back to the wheel slot just before starting home from the ice pack. Ralph didn't like the demotion, but he really wasn't lead dog material.

When I gave the word, Tanya at once swung around and lunged into her harness, almost dragging

156

the slower Wolf.   When the other dogs didn't respond quickly enough, she turned, giving a growl deep in her throat.   This time they followed, and we shot back across the glazed surface of the ocean.

The sun had now become a red glow in the south above the Brooks Range.   The ice formations, the sky, the dogs—everything was tinged and saturated with the pinkish orange Arctic glow.   And the glow seemed to come from within the ice, giving depth to the surface.   On clear ice, it seemed that we skated on a wisp of air above a flashing pit of pink fire.

The Arctic ice pack—no wonder men like Peary and Amundsen devoted their lives to exploring it.   What a strange feeling to know you could just turn the dogs around and, by travelling far enough, eventually hit the northern tip of Greenland.

Darkness fell swiftly on the team, followed by the pre-rising glow of the moon.   The dogs appeared in front as stately trotting silhouettes doing a frozen minuet against the sky.   I paused with my head on the driving bow, and gave thanks for the experience.   We had become one with Nature. . . . one with the world . . . I no longer had just eleven dogs and a sled.

I had a team.

25

Before the sunlight had broken through the Brooks Range to the south all the dogs had been harnessed, and the five-hundred pounds of gear secured to the sled.

The temperature was a calm minus fifteen degrees. The peaks of the Brooks Range could be seen as the distant wall of a room, with the ever-present overcast for a ceiling.

After a last-minute check, I swung the leaders around onto the road and they rushed south toward Valdez.

We were to follow an ice road for twenty-five miles to the south, to a core-drilling site. From there on south, it was unbroken snow and river ice until Sagwon, some eighty miles distant. Sagwon consisted of a mobile home sitting next to an airstrip. It would seem a paradise.

But we were not to start the trip that day.

About two miles from camp, one of the men from our camp stood out on the road, waving wildly for us to stop. I yelled to him to grab the leaders, and I put all my weight on the ineffectual brake. A brake works well on snow, but ice won't let it grip. He dove for the dogs, and was dragged a short way before they became tangled and stopped. I helped him get free and asked him what was up.

"You've gotta turn back," he said, out of breath. "There's a storm due any minute, and the boss says it'll be a howler."

"You can't be right!" I told him. "Look at the mountains—clear as a bell!"

"I know it don't seem right," he said, his Texas drawl showing, "but they're calling everyone in from the rigs. I'm not kidding. I took a big chance coming to get y'all."

It still didn't seem logical, but I decided to play it safe. He helped me turn the team around, which took about fifteen seconds, and as I turned my back on the leaders, I felt the snappy crisp of ice fog at my face.

Looking up, I saw the curtain of fog ring down on the Brooks Range in seconds. There was a sense of quietly whirling coolness, and the world turned gray.

Everyone has seen fog, but this fog came on with-

159

out warning. By the time I walked back to the sled, most of the dog team had been swallowed by the swirling veils. I grabbed the driving bow, yelled to the dogs, and we churned off into a bleak whiteout.

Twelve feet in front of me, the tails of the wheel dogs appeared as faintly moving brushes. Everything ahead of those tails had been swallowed.

Behind me, not more than three feet away, were the headlights of the pick-up truck. There was no longer any road. There was nothing but the fog and an increasing wind. Somewhere ahead in the whiteout, Wolf and Tanya were running on raw instinct back to camp. There was no choice but to trust them—completely.

Then, the small threatenings of wind became a full-blown storm. It didn't appear to have much direction. It just was. It was all around, blowing down, up, and from all four points of the compass. The force was so strong I had to turn my head sideways to breathe, and the exposed flesh on my face was freezing fast. In attempting to talk, I discovered I couldn't move my jaw muscles. Clinging to the driving bow, I crouched down to lessen wind resistance.

After what seemed an endless trip, the dogs stopped and curled up. I found it hard to believe. We must be fairly close to camp, and yet they would quit us. Hanging tightly to the tow line, I worked my way forward hand-over-hand to the leaders. Wolf came in sight, bathed by a glow of light. Tanya was curled up. Two feet above her head was a door handle. I was on the porch at camp. The light above Wolf's head was a football stadium light, but was barely visible twenty feet away.

Working back to the sled, I motioned to the truck driver, and together we plugged in the truck and chained the dogs. When we finally stepped through the door to the false porch, we began silly hoarse laughing at each other's appearance. We were both so covered with frost, it appeared we had been dipped in water and placed in a freezer.

When my friend tried to talk, with his face muscles frozen, it sounded strange, but the words were okay.

"Son," he said, with true southern hospitality, "I'm going to buy you a cup of coffee!"

Inside the building was Dr. Felt, who had been paying the camp a routine visit when the ground blizzard hit. Several men were stranded in the rigs, and would be stuck there until the storm abated. We raised them on the radio, and they were comfortable. All of the equipment used by men on the Slope was well provisioned with emergency rations, blankets, sleeping bags, and paperback novels. The custom-made gas tanks held enough fuel to keep the engines going for several days.

It snows less than one level foot each year on the Arctic Slope. The present storm, and others like it that occur with some frequency, are ground blizzards, the Arctic equivalent to a desert sandstorm. The wind simply picks up what snow there is, and redistributes it at hurricane velocity here and there.

The men caught in the equipment don't seem to mind. In fact, they are given overtime pay for each hour spent away from camp, and at times the storms last for three days.

The men stuck in Crazyhorse Camp weren't so pleased with the confinement. Although they were warm, well-fed, and had plenty of entertainment, there is one serious drawback to being stormed in anywhere in Alaska. The problem may have a psychology textbook name, but is commonly called cabin fever up here. It can only be cured by a pleasant day.

While the fever runs its course, however, there are misunderstandings, break-ups of forty-year partnerships, divorce, and the end of domestic tranquillity. On rare occasions, it has proven terminal. How many deaths in the bush result from cabin fever would be impossible to ascertain. Occasionally, a trapper has shown up in town in spring, reporting that "poor old Joe" went through a hole in the ice. Maybe Joe did, and maybe he was helped. Nobody would know but his partner.

Normally, the men are quite happy to sit inside the camp building and play the usual game of poker, listen to the Buck Owens tapes, or shoot pool. They can stay like that for days, happily, because they know they can get in a truck and get a change of scene. If they have had enough of Slope life, they can jump in the big bird and fly south for some sun.

During a storm, though, the camp takes on an entirely different meaning. The buildings then become just as much a prison cell as a submarine under twenty fathoms of water. There is no possibility of survival for a man exposed for any length of time outside the building. The stories of men who have left the camps during a storm to walk one-hundred yards to another building—and died before reaching it—are too numerous to arouse any wanderlust in the men. Those things have happened.

On this particular evening, one of the geologists, a college man, got in a heated debate with a former Fairbanks policeman on the subject of civil disobedience. The argument drew a small crowd of men (there were about fifteen men in camp at that time), who added their two cents. The college man may have had some good points, but he was outgunned, called them all "uneducated slobs", and went to drink some coffee.

Two men began playing ping pong. After two serves, one of the men missed an easy return, slammed the paddle down on the table, and went to his room.

Smokey's tape deck, usually a major enjoyment, drew strong criticism. A hot discussion comparing Buck Owens to Marty Robbins and Hank Thompson, ended (surprisingly) with Beethoven, Chopin, and Berlioz.

Nobody even mentioned the possibility of the nightly poker game.

I finally pulled up a cup of coffee and joined Dr. Felt at one of the tables.

"I've been thinking, Slim," he said, "that you really ought to shave off your beard."

At once I was indignant, and wanted to know why.

"Because in extreme cold, beards can be quite dangerous."

I mentioned that a number of the men on the Slope had beards.

"That's true," he said, "but they are never out in the cold for more than a few minutes at a time, as a rule. They leave the camp building and jump into a heated pick-up truck. They drive the truck to an

164

enclosed, heated drilling rig, where the temperature is about sixty above. You'll be exposed to extreme cold for days at a stretch. You'd better prepare for that."

"But why the beard?"

"Beards hold ice from your breath, and then freeze your face. The whiskers hide the blotches of frostbite from you. They add almost no insulation at all."

He added that the old adage about taking a flask of whisky, a fat woman, and growing a beard in cold weather were two-thirds wrong. In fact, he said, the beard and the liquor were the two most dangerous things to do in the cold besides leaving your parka home.

"Besides the beard's problems," he said, "alcohol dilates the blood vessels, making you sweat more, which speeds up the heat loss from the body. If you sweat, and then get chilled, you can freeze twice as quickly."

Doc gave me a small booklet issued to all men on the Slope concerning extreme cold.

"Most of the men never open this book," he said, "and chances are they won't be in a position to need all this information. But you should memorize this thing. It could save your life."

Doc added one more note of advice.

"If you feel yourself becoming slightly drunk

after being in the cold for a long time, just do your best to stay warm. Cold will slow the flow of blood to the brain as well as the extremities, and a lack of oxygen can cause drunkenness the same as a diver gets 'rapture of the deep' or an alcoholic gets his stupor. Just get warm as quickly as you can. Your judgement will be impaired just as though you'd gone on a bender. It can lead to a coma, and then death, if you don't do anything about it."

Doc failed to mention the other third of that old adage, but I didn't know any fat women anyway. I thanked him and went to my room to lie down and read. After reading descriptions of freezing to death (known as hypothermia), I went to the shower room and shaved off my beard.

It had been a good beard, and had gone many places with me—but a new beard is easier to come by than a new face.

Sometime quietly in the night the wind died, the storm lifted to its constant hovering, and the morning was beautiful.

26

It was an ideal day for mushing, and we were harnessed and gone as soon as it was light enough. The weather was absolutely perfect: five below, no wind, overcast, and about one-hundred-mile visibility. The white prominences of the Brooks loomed far to the south.

The team responded eagerly to Tanya's opening lunge, and loped the first two miles down the hard-packed ice road. Twenty-five miles away was the drilling rig, which we hoped to make that day.

When their initial burst of energy had been used up, they settled into the swinging freight trot which sled dogs have used since the Malemiut Eskimos on the Yukon's mouth first domesticated the wolf.

All I had to do was stand on the sled, watch the unending snow flow swiftly and quietly by, and enjoy the ride. I have always excelled at that.

The dogs responded to little cheers of encouragement, keeping the sled moving at about ten miles per hour. They would slow down a little, later in the day, but they were working as a team, and were putting long cold miles behind us.

The North Slope is as flat as a billiard table, but actually rises unnoticed gradually as you travel south. After an hour's mushing, the tower lights from the airstrip disappeared and two small mounds loomed on either side of the road in front of us.

Geologists say that these strange mounds, which rise straight up for ten to fifteen feet, and occasionally higher, above the tundra, are pressure bumps from the permafrost. The frozen counterparts of volcanoes, they mark the weak spots where pressure from below forces a hill. To the Eskimo, however, they were shoved up in loving handfuls by a gracious God who wanted to give the people a vantage point for caribou hunting. The Eskimo word for these tiny hills is *pingaluk*. As usual, the name was changed for the benefit of the oilmen to pingoes.

Reaching the pingoes, I thought I might try the little walkie-talkie for the sake of good honest fun. It was carried, along with a flashlight, strobe light, rescue locator beacon, and my camera, in a knapsack on my chest and inside my parka for warmth.

I pulled the antennae, flipped the switch, and

168

yelled, "Dog Team One to Crazy Horse"—they had given me a class calling name—"Dog Team One to Crazy Horse!"

That there was no "Dog Team Two" for at least two hundred miles didn't change my elation at being number one.

Bill, one of the men back in camp, quickly answered, and asked how I was doing. I told him, and then said I had just then passed between the two pingoes on the road. Could he give me my location?

To my surprise (and his, I imagine), he said just over fifteen miles!

Never had the miles gone so quickly. We had been on trail then not quite an hour and a half. Bill said I would soon come in sight of the Franklin Bluffs, and said the drilling site was just about even with the center of them. He would radio the drilling site and tell them to expect me.

Soon the flat top of the bluffs grew out of the flat white horizon. It was a pleasure to see some change in the unbroken whiteness of the landscape. I was struck at how closely it resembled the buttes I'd seen in the deserts of Arizona and New Mexico. They rose straight up from the tundra, notched by tiny vertical arroyos, with a broad flat expanse on top. The top of the bluffs were, I would guess, about ten miles long and three wide.

The top stood perhaps five-hundred feet above the level of the tundra.

The men at camp had told me I would be likely to see wolves and moose near the bluffs, as there are a few willows in the draws, and handy rockpiles for wolf dens.

As we drew alongside the north end of the bluffs, two of the dogs looked quickly to the right and whined. I couldn't see anything but snow. Then one snowball after another took flight, and I counted ten ptarmigan that had risen from a point only six feet from the sled.

During the hours of travel on the road, I had practically nothing to do. If I had had a harmonica, it would have been a good time to practice. As it was, I recited the "Cremation of Sam McGee", which I had once memorized to amaze family and friends, and daydreamed about the girls in Anchorage.

Every now and then, I'd take out the camera, or one of the electronic gizmos, and fiddle with it. Finally I reached the drilling site on the radio. Dr. Dave Sanders, the geologist in charge of the operation, informed me I must be within five miles of the site, as that was all the strength his radio had.

A few more quick-trotting minutes, and I spotted the portable derrick in a sea of white. Vehicle headlights lighted the scene, where men were drilling the soil samples. One of the men honked a horn when he saw the team crest the slight rise and slide into the shallow valley toward the flats along the Sagavaanirktok River.

We would be following the course of the "Sag" River upstream, to its headwaters at Dietrich Pass.

There are several popular theories about how the Sagavaanirktok River got its name.

One concerns the famous German explorer Count Gustav Mahler Van Irktok. It seems the poor fellow had planned to hunt the rare equatorial pocket gopher in Colombia, but there had been a mix-up with the travel agent, and he found himself at Prudhoe Bay with a butterfly net and a hammock with mosquito netting.

Determined to make the best of an honest mistake, however, the good Count snagged a wayward lemming with the net, and was immediately dragged into the ocean and drowned.

In story and legend around a thousand campfires the "Saga of Van Irktok" was recounted, and the river near where he drowned was given its name.

Not so, say the Eskimos. According to them, the river had been named centuries before the German had set foot in Alaska, and by bands of wandering Eskimo caribou hunters. Sagavaanirktok, in Inupiat Eskimo, they tell us, means "Water-where-crazy-cheechakoes-will-someday-drill-for-oil."

The controversy rages on in scientific and exploratory journals, but the oilmen have solved the problem by corrupting the river's name to Sag.

It was beginning to get dark now, and the dogs were pretty tired. Their trot had slowed considerably, and I began to do a lot of pumping to help them along. Thankfully, they all seemed in good health and spirits, and were pulling well after a twenty-five-mile run. I was proud of them, but tired as we pulled the final hundred yards to the rigs.

Then they saw the fox.

The little white Arctic foxes of this region are everywhere, and have become quite tame. They resemble a Pomeranian dog, all white, with a black button nose and black eyes. Since the men on the Slope are not allowed firearms, they have done the next best thing, and have made pets of them.

Each man takes a huge lunch with him each day. Their appetites are not that hearty, but the little foxes enjoy the leftovers. This particular fox (his name was Joey) had been lunching on a roast beef sandwich when the team came in sight. He quickly scampered across the road and out into the snowfields as hard as he could. Tanya and Wolf spotted him first and gave chase, followed by nine others. The little fellow promised good sport, and they shot after him at a full run.

As we flew past the men on the rig, I just waved, jamming the ineffectual brake onto the hard surface. When we left the road and started out into softer snow, the brake became effective, and we rolled up a monstrous pile of snow beneath the sled, finally bringing the team to a stop.

Dave Sanders ran out and helped me turn the team around, then he drove them to the site as I watched. With the men's help, the team was soon picketed and fed.

Glancing at my watch, I found that we had covered the twenty-five miles in four hours and ten minutes. The ice road extended only five miles beyond the drilling site, and would leave me with the river ice on the Sag, and unbroken trail through soft snow, so I wasn't counting on making much better time.

Sanders talked me into coming back to camp with the men that night, assuring me that the night crew would keep an eye on the dogs. We drove back in the dark, and I fell asleep in the back of the truck, listening to stories of drinking bouts in Fairbanks, and the glories of the girls in Anchorage.

173

27

The dogs were barking and wagging the next morning when I arrived with the day crew. They were harnessed and snapped into place quickly, and the sled was relashed. I had developed a system for keeping the dogs from becoming tangled in their pre-lunge frenzy. Eskimos using this many dogs for a team usually had a family member to help hold the dogs, but, being alone, I had to try a different tack. The heavy sled was anchored by a large iron snow anchor (hook), and a second anchor was tied on a six-foot rope and fastened to the collar of one of the leaders. Stretching the rigging out as far as it would go, I stomped this second anchor firmly into the snow.

Sometimes, the leader would pull up the front anchor, and mosey around through the crowd, creating an unholy mess of dogs, harness, tug lines, and fights. But it worked this morning, and we headed south along the remnant of the ice road. It was fifteen degrees below zero, and my glasses fogged and immediately froze. By this time, a breeze was blowing from the north, just enough to make the cold even colder. As it was at our backs, though, we didn't mind it.

While we loped along, I thought of one very popular novel concerning Canadian Eskimos, written by a man who had, no doubt, never been north of Phoenix. It depicted an Eskimo family driving south across the polar sea to a trading post by dog team. The author said the poor Eskimo family had to strip to the buff due to the "unusually extreme heat" of fifteen below! I know an awful lot of Eskimos, and when the temperature drops below zero, they wear parka and mittens like everyone else. A naked man at fifteen below would very soon die of exposure, and I don't care *what* culture he was reared in. These published fountainheads of misinformation are not only widely read and accepted, but are highly praised by the critics.

Fifteen below is cold—even to an Eskimo.

The frost problem with my glasses, though, was something early Eskimos didn't have to contend with. Time after time, I would stop the team, pull off my heavy Air Force mittens, and scrape the

175

lenses with a fingernail through my light gloves. This operation is much like scraping a frosty car windshield with a comb. Finally, two little windows would appear in the glass, and we would continue south until they became obscured.

As we progressed, Wolf had shown a definite reluctance to share the lead spot with Tanya (or anyone, save for passive Ralph) so I put him back in swing with Prince, giving Tanya the solo lead spot. She thrived on it.

At the end of the road, Tanya quickly swung east toward the river, plunging over a six-foot berm, and led the team across the snowfield. I pushed the sled up the berm, reached the point of balance, then jumped on the runners as it swooped down the other side. To my surprise and pleasure, the wind that morning had coated the snow with a two-inch crust, and the dogs and sled traveled easily across the top without crashing through to the powder.

Here's the funny thing about those crusts. When I would put one foot off the sled to "peddle" a little, my foot would break through, but the twelve-foot sled, with well over six-hundred pounds (including my weight) on it, would glide smoothly across the top, sinking less than an inch into the crust.

About mid-day, I noticed a marked nervousness in the dogs as we neared the frozen Sagavaanirktok

River. They would look over to the left as they trotted along, and several dogs whimpered occasionally. For about an hour, I failed to find the source of their discomfort. Finally, I made out three dark shapes moving along parallel with us, and about three-hundred yards away.

Wolves!

There is an international misconception about wolves. Their fame as plunderers of big game and devourers of trappers reads well in Jack London's stories, but the truth is a lot farther away. For the record, there has never been a single instance of a wolf attacking a human being in North America. Not one. I had no fear of being the first.

The reason for their interested inspection of the team wasn't difficult to understand, either. One of my dogs, Snoopy, a pretty little white Samoyed, had come in heat several days ago. It was more than likely her exuding romance through the air that drew the spectators.

At that time, Alaska still had a bounty on wolves, fifty dollars a head, and I carried a rifle. But it was much more fun to watch them trot along, sometimes playfully romping with each other, as they trailed the caravan of strangers through their hunting territory.

After stopping for lunch, we plunged down a steep bank, and careened out onto the smooth ice of the Sag River. In the Arctic, the country looks much the same all over, but so long as we remained on the river, there was no getting lost. The ice was blown fairly free of snow, and the broad frozen highway wound south into the Brooks Range.

As it grew dark, I looked for likely places to build an igloo. Suddenly, Tanya left the broad river ice and began churning up the west bank of the river through deep snow. At first, I thought I had another Prince on my hands. Why leave the path of least resistance to flounder in deep drifts?

Stopping the team, I tried to turn Tanya back onto the ice, but she cried and frantically redoubled her efforts to leave. I left the team and began walking ahead of her tracks up the river. After covering about fifty yards, the ice began to crackle beneath my mukluks, with water seeping through into the open air.

This was overflow.

As the ice covering on a river grows thicker, it also grows heavier. It pushes down on the still-liquid river with increasing force until a small weakness in the ice gives way to a crack, and fresh water bubbles up through it, and begins spreading around on the surface. Due to the constant movement of the shallow surface water, the ice covering is thin, and a person, or dog team, can break through, wetting their feet thoroughly. As overflow continues throughout the long winter, rivers grow to be three

178

or four times their summer width by spring, and can spell quick death to travelers.

In extreme cold, a wet foot can cause death. If a dog's foot gets wet, it must be dried and warmed immediately by rubbing it dry and then putting as much of the paw as possible into your mouth or armpit. I suppose it's possible, as was once suggested to me, to put two husky feet into the musher's armpits, but that person could never have tried to get a ninety-pound dog to comply.

If a man gets his foot wet in sub-zero weather, his only chance is to build a fire immediately, take off the wet clothes, and dry them out. On the Slope, there is no firewood, so a man's feet had better stay dry.

While I was thankful for Tanya's vigilance in keeping us out of the overflow, I was also baffled. When she veered off the trail, there was no over- flow. How could she have known it was com- ing? And why did she turn off at all? The ice on top of the overflow was strong enough to hold a dog. Only the musher and the sled would have cracked the crust and gotten wet.

Near the west bank of the river, I found a snow- drift for igloo construction. After the dogs were picketed and fed, I quickly pitched the old army mountain tent behind the sled. This was in the event the weather changed before I could erect a snowhouse.

Using a snowshoe, I tunnelled into the snowbank for a way and found the snow fairly moist and easy to compact. Then I began setting up my blocks in a rough circle (any Canadian Eskimo could make this one look sick) and capped it off with a roof made of snowshoe rafters and tarp top. I piled snow on the tarp to seal it. It takes a great deal of time to complete the traditional spiral dome of an igloo, and my modification worked just as well for an overnight camp.

Pulling inside what I'd need for the night, I scooped up snow for a sleeping bench, and laid the bedding out along it. On the floor (slightly lower than the bench), the cooking gear was arranged, the little Coleman puffer humming happily, and the place began to look like home. The one-burner pressure fuel stove gave light as well as heat, as the snow walls reflect a lot of light from the small flames.

There are two cardinal rules in igloo building. Number One: always leave a hole in the room for ventilation, and a crack in the tunnel entrance. This is quickly done with the sharp tail of a snowshoe or a ski pole. The best place seems to be above the crawl hole, as both are on the lee side of the snow house, and the breeze will create a suction for the fumes.

Number Two: Care must be taken that the occupant doesn't melt his house. It may be twenty

180

below outside, but once the igloo is enclosed, the temperature is around the freezing point. Ice appears to be more resistant to melting than snow, so my *modus operandi* was to fire the stove up good and hot for about ten minutes. This started the snow walls melting and running into otherwise unchinked cracks. Then I would shut the stove off until the inside was well frozen again. After the stove was rekindled, I kept the flames low. The ingenious Eskimo shelter stays remarkably warm, and a quite comfortable night can be spent. I always check the ventilation shaft several times each night to reassure myself that it's open. But it was just more worry on my part, as I haven't had to reopen one yet.

Igloo, incidentally, is the Inupiat word for "house"—an entirely different word is used for the snow house in Alaska. The Alaskan Eskimos have never lived in igloos on a long-term basis, but use them only occasionally as overnight shelters while hunting. Their ancestral winter home was a driftwood and turf combination closely resembling the Navajo hogan. In Canada, however, the igloo was the winter house of the people.

Inside, I was snug, and soon had snow melting for tea, followed by dehydrated food for dinner. Outside, under a cold cloudy sky, the dogs had done exactly as I did. They burrowed down into the snow, let the wind blow snow over them, and kept a small hole open with their noses. Huskies do this instinctively, but end up with exactly the same type of shelter that I had made. They stay warm, too, at the coldest temperatures.

Tomorrow, I would be traveling again on the snow, as travel on the river ice (at least for this stretch) was out of the question. We had made about fifteen miles that day, as nearly as I could figure, and would be pleased if we could keep up that pace. It was nice to think about as I ate slowly and thankfully.

Making my daily entry in the small log book, I crawled in the sleeping bag and turned off the stove. Before falling asleep, pictures of the first igloo I had built flooded my mind.

Alaska is green in the summer, but I was determed to practice building igloos before necessity demanded it. Eklutna Glacier sits up a steep canyon about thirty miles from Anchorage. I planned a weekend trip with a friend of mine and a young man from one of the large cities Outside who begged to come along.

As the three of us made our way up the steep face of the glacier, my buddy (another dog musher) and I began to warn our cheechako friend of some of the dangerous animals living in the area.

Of course, the most ferocious animal in Alaska is the mosquito, and we were having a bout with them at the time, but we brought up another (and much rarer) beast for our friend. To be kind, we'll call him Bob.

"Yes, Bob," we said, "the only thing you have to watch for up here is a glacier snake."

"Glacier snake?"

"Yeah," my partner said, with a straight face, "you must have heard of them in the scientific journals at school."

"No."

"Well, you *have* heard of the ice worms on the glaciers, haven't you?"

"Somebody mentioned them to me on the plane coming up . . ."

"Right. Well, these used to be ice worms, but with the atomic testing at Amchitka and all, enough radiation leaked to the glaciers up here that the ice worms mutated . . . giving us glacier snakes."

"No kidding?"

"Yeah, but there's not much to worry about. . . . really. An independent study proved conclusively that only one person in ten who visits the glaciers dies of their bite."

By this time, Bob was fairly excited. We found a good place where the snow had stayed cold in a fissure, and began building our snow house.

"There's nothing to worry about, Bob. Just think of the statistics."

The results of the independent study didn't seem to be assuaging his fears by much, however, and he openly asked why we didn't seem worried about them.

"Well," we said, "the truth is, the snakes only seem to go after people who haven't been up here very long. It's probably because a resident's body temperature is much lower than that of a person from Outside."

"I never knew that!"

"Sure," we lied, "otherwise we wouldn't be able to take the cold up here in the winter."

"Oh, I see."

"Yeah, so when the snake crawls into a sleeping bag with someone at night, he's just naturally going to choose the warmest person he can find."

His face had turned the same pale blue as the glacier by this time.

"Isn't there any way to keep them out of camp?" Bob asked.

My partner said, "The only way I know is to set up a snake ring around camp."

He asked how it was done, and my partner began to explain. (I was more than a little curious myself.)

My partner then carefully told how, by employing a certain bodily function in a circle around the camp, the snakes won't cross it.

184

We had to finish building the igloo by ourselves. Bob was busy melting snow for water over the stove and drinking tea. When we finished dinner, the yellow ring extended nearly halfway around camp. We told him to be careful and not leave any bare spots, as a snake can crawl through a very small gap in the line. He drank more tea.

We went to bed early that night, tired from the hike, but I don't think Bob got any sleep at all. He was still fixing tea when I got up in the middle of the night to help with his snake ring (he later complained about my arc) and shortly switched to Kool-Aid for something different.

I woke briefly later that night when I heard him shoving the entrance block out to leave.

"Anything wrong?" I asked.

"Two feet to go!" he answered.

And that was how I learned to build igloos, such as the one I was then falling asleep in on the Arctic Slope.

28

The deep diesel bawl of a wolf, joined by another in a higher pitch, woke me before dawn.   I lighted the Coleman burner and fixed tea and ham for breakfast.

It was Friday, November 20, and the world outside the igloo was white and dark at the same time—and very cold.   Listening to the radio transmissions between the camps with my walkie-talkie, I learned it was twenty-five below at Sagwon, my destination for the day.

At twenty below and colder, there seems to be a definite feel in the air that isn't noticed at warmer temperatures.   It is a total chill, as though a man left a sauna and stepped into a cold storage plant.   At this temperature, exposed flesh freezes in sixty seconds, so the trick is not to expose any flesh.   My full-knit hood was again put into play, with the addition of a "Slope mask" given me by the foreman at Crazy Horse Camp. It is a felt-lined leather mask, with slots for the mouth and eyes.

It took a while to reconvert the roof of the igloo into tarp and snowshoes, and load and lash the gear on the sled. It was beginning to turn pink in the south as I walked along the picket chain, retrieving the dogs. By morning, all that's visible on the picket line are eleven little geysers of warm breath emerging through finger-sized holes. The musher must reach down through the snow at each geyser, grab the submerged dog, and pull him, unwilling and shivering, into the cold air.

With the team harnessed, I walked ahead of Tanya with snowshoes, packing a trail through the soft snow. Unlike experienced freight teams, however, they didn't know enough to follow me, and I was forced to walk back to the team and drive them forward to the end of the packed trail. Then it was back to the front again, and pack more trail.

After half a mile of this, we reached a slight rise in the snow, where the wind had blown a good crust. Off came the snowshoes, and the team struck off at a good trot across the glazed surface while a tired musher rode the runners. The break came just in time to save my flagging spirits, because breaking trail is tough work, and I wasn't used to the awkward shuffling gait necessary with the big twelve-by-sixty snowshoes.

The dogs picked up some speed across the glaze, pulling away from the south buttress of the Franklin Bluffs. Shortly, through the expanse of white, some gently rolling hills began to show up ahead. These I knew to be the Sag Hills, the northernmost foothills of the Brooks Range. Reaching them was a particularly tasty goal for me. When we reached the base of those hills, we would have accomplished the first solo dog sled crossing of the North Slope at that longitude. I urged the dogs on further and faster.

Gazing down the long towline ahead of me, I checked on each dog's progress in the team. For once, all eleven dogs were running without a tangle across the glaze, and seemed to enjoy it.

Then I noticed something strange about George . . .

George, a pretty Siberian named for champion musher George Attla, had begun to weave drunkenly in his traces. Then he hung back in his harness for a second and flopped on his side.

I slammed on the brake, and jammed the hook into the snow. Running to the young dog, I unsnapped him from the neckline so he wouldn't choke, and picked him up. There was no breath in him, his eyes had begun to glaze, and the usually pink flesh of the mouth showed traces of cyanotic blue. I rolled him over in my arms and began to

188

blow into his mouth. It was hard to make a seal around his mouth with the heavy mittens on, so I pulled them off and tried again. This helped quite a bit. With my bare hands, I was able to make a much better seal around the long pointed muzzle.

Trying not to hurry, as feelings of panic and regret engulfed me, I continued for long steady minutes with the resuscitation.

Feeling a cold nose in my face, I looked up to see Doc, George's partner, whining and looking anxiously at what I was doing.

Doc was a big square-jawed cross between a husky and a St. Bernard (as nearly as I could guess) and he and George had become close partners. Doc was named for Dr. Roland Lombard, who in real life is the friend and perennial mushing rival of George Attla.

My left hand, totally exposed to the cold for long minutes, now began to stiffen. Unwillingly, I laid the dead body of the little Siberian on the snow and forced my frozen hand back into the mitten.

But the hand didn't hurt, and wasn't on my mind. I was hurt and angry at the injustice of this dog's death. At least when Scarface died, there was a reason. George, a young dog, had pulled and felt good, and had shown no signs of sickness until a very few seconds before his death.

Just as I laid him down, there was a hum in the

sky, and the big Wien jet streaked with its low drone toward Prudhoe Bay.   Aboard that warm airplane, pretty girls would be serving coffee to lounging people.   At my feet lay the lifeless form of a little sled dog.   My tears froze to my face.

Removing his harness and collar, I kicked a hole in the snow, tumbled the remains in, and covered it as best I could.   The ravens would find it anyway, but I'd at least make them work for it.

An hour's mushing later, the glazed surface disappeared, and the lead dogs floundered in powder snow three feet deep.   By now, we had swung in an arc, carrying us close to the Sag River again.   The hills were upon us, and we would take the river or its edge along the side of the hills until we reached the crossing to Sagwon.   From the soft miasmas of fog rising from the river, it was obvious that overflow still existed, ruling out a return to the ice.

Strapping on the snowshoes, I set out ahead of the team, stomping the soft powder as hard as I could. My heavy clothes, and the constant trodding work, soon had me gasping for breath. The steam from my body rose out through the openings in the winter gear, and hung in a frozen vapor around my body as I went.

Pack, pack, pack . . .

The work went on.   I would break trail for several hundred yards, then return to the team and

190

drive them the short distance to powder snow again. Then the snowshoer went back to his task.

Pack, pack, pack . . .

The vibrato of a helicopter interrupted my work, and I looked up to see the familiar Bell Jetranger of the pipeline camps. I welcomed the opportunity to rest for a few minutes. Pulling out my walkie-talkie, I talked to the pilot, who asked if I was all right. He put my position as being about nine miles north of Sagwon.

"You're right on course," he said. "We thought we'd land for a minute."

"Come ahead," I said.

What I wanted right then was a cold drink of water, but the thermos of hot coffee they brought more than made up for the lack of water. Two men aboard the chopper took pictures of the team while I told the pilot of George's death.

"I'll fly over tomorrow again," the pilot promised, "but you'll probably make Sagwon tonight."

"I sure hope so," I said, "but there's a lot of trail to break first."

"Well, good luck," they said.

The jet engine began its whine, grew louder, and the snow blew up in huge clouds around the machine. The dogs turned their backs to the prop-wash as they would on a storm, and the chopper lifted lazily into the air and hummed south toward

Happy Valley Camp, eighteen miles south of Sagwon.

When this sole reminder of the modern world had vanished, it left a very lonely feeling behind. All about was just a quiet white world. The total silence and distance had an almost narcotic effect. More and more, the team and I seemed to be miserable ants, crawling across a belligerent white cold surface.

Back I went to the snowshoes. Pack, pack, pack . . .

When I returned to the team this time, they all began sniffing the air with nervous agitation. Driving the dogs, I noticed a reluctance of many of them to move at all. This seemed quite strange, as we hadn't gone far enough that day for them to be tired. Tanya especially was hesitant about going. She finally yielded to my command, and walked quietly and slowly, looking from side to side. Sometimes she'd stop and stick her nose in the air. Most of the team followed after her.

Finally she quit. She just looked back at me once, then began digging a hole in the snow. Several others began to follow her actions.

Walking ahead, I grabbed Tanya and tried to drag her forward. Not only would she not take a step, but none of the nine dogs behind her would, either. It is possible to drag one eighty-five-pound dog, but not ten of them.   The minute I released her, she went back to digging her hole in the snow.   All the others were doing the same by this time, so there was no sense in trying to go any farther.

I spread out the picket chains, then unharnessed and dragged each dog to the chain.   As soon as they had been fastened, they dug frantically under the snow.   Had I been a bit smarter, I would have paid more attention, but I begrudgingly went about my tent staking and unloading of the sled, thinking of warm Sagwon, now a scant eight miles away, and the bed and food that waited there.

The temperature dropped remarkably fast, and I noticed the exposed noses of the dogs were covered with thick frost.   My breath drifted to the sled, and froze to it.   It was becoming painful to breathe.

Then I noticed the total absence of sound.   It was the deliberate silence of the North—the stunned, half-quivering silence of the theatre audience as the house lights dim.

Moving in silent haste, I shoved my sleeping bag and valuables into the tent, and turned to begin my igloo, but I did it with a crawling fear.   Something was going to happen.   The stage was set, the audience was afraid of the outcome.   I felt the fear rising inside, and cursed myself for the weakness.

Then the storm hit.

29

The whiteout dropped first, obscuring the dogs, and concentrating the range of vision to the tent and the sled. It was silent and deliberate as it went about its work, concealing its coming deeds from the eyes of the world.

I stood there for the few seconds it took to drop, watching it swallow my dogs and the front part of the sled.

The first blast of wind tumbled me into a snow-drift and snapped one of the tent poles like a twig. Gasping for breath, I quickly shed the snow-shoes, and used one of them to replace the broken tent pole. Then I crawled into the tiny tunnel-flap on the lee side of the tent. Pulling off my mukluks, I crawled into the six-pound down sleeping bag, which was guaranteed to minus seventy degrees.

When the initial shock of the blast had worn off, I searched through my duffle bag and found the

194

Coleman burner, then pulled out some dehydrated food for dinner. I could only keep my hands unmittened for a few seconds each time, as the cold would go quickly through the light "monkey face" gloves and freeze them.

When I tried to pump and light the burner, nothing happened. I shook it, but just heard a sludgy sloshing inside. When the reservoir was opened, I poured out a few lumps of white gas in a form resembling catsup. Later, other Alaskans told me that Blazo does this at minus forty, but I had to learn the hard way.

Fishing again in the duffle bag, I located several cans of Sterno that I had brought along on a whim. It was fortunate that I did, for the Sterno began to burn immediately, and did well for the several hours that it lasted.

It was most difficult heating anything over the Sterno, due to the difference in temperature between the bottom of the pan and the top. Nevertheless, I was able to melt snow and get the water at least warm, then soak the dried food in it, making it chewy. Several hours later, dinner of soggy crunchy beef and noodles, and three bars of chocolate was completed. I washed it down with lukewarm water just as the last of the Sterno burned away.

The wind picked up. It blew on the tent until I

felt sure we would all be blown to Greenland, but enough snow had drifted around the tent by this time that it was held down firmly.

In fact, holding down the tent created one of my biggest problems. With the tent walls crushing down, space was becoming nonexistent. I couldn't afford to get buried by the storm, as certain suffocation would follow.

How long would the storm last?

The one I had been caught in at Deadhorse lasted fifteen hours, but the men kept saying we were overdue for a good blow. A "blow" in this country sometimes lasts five and six days, with the average storm lasting about three days.

As if that weren't enough, I began to notice a light layer of powdery snow covering the duffle and my other gear inside the tent. Looking down toward my feet, I discovered the source. A tiny hole on the windward side of the tent, smaller than a pencil puncture, was allowing a fine spray of snow inside. It resembled the spray from an aerosol can. It was located too far up the tent wall for me to plug it with some gear, so I draped a piece of tarp over most of my gear.

By keeping the flashlight, walkie-talkie, and rescue gear inside my sleeping bag, I could keep the batteries warm enough to work.

Every hour or so, I would turn on the walkie-talkie, carefully poking the antenna out the breathing hole of my sleeping bag. Until late that night, I heard nothing.

At about one a.m., I picked up a radio signal. Happy Valley Camp was calling Crazy Horse.

They spoke for several minutes about what machinery the one camp needed from the other, and then they mentioned the weather.

"How is it at your place?" one said.

"Blowin' bad," said the other, "about forty-five below with sixty-knot winds gusting to around eighty."

"Yeah," said the first, "dropped to minus fifty for about an hour, but is back to forty-five now."

Then they signed off, and left the tent in silence. Having a pretty good memory of the chill factor chart, I knew that the rating didn't go that low. Wind drops the temperature of an area at a certain rate. Wind robs the body of heat much more quickly in cold weather. Therefore, when it is zero degrees with a ten-mile-per-hour wind, the weather chills a person as much as though it were calm outside and twenty below. A person will freeze as quickly in that circumstance as he would at the lower temperature.

The chart goes down to minus 148 degrees, and the storm outside went beyond. It doesn't matter, though, because at chill factors of 148 below, which is 180 degrees of frost, flesh will freeze almost immediately, and the lungs get seared by the forced cold, causing death.

At first, the storm seemed rather exciting Unlike the Sergeant Preston programs, though, the wind doesn't whistle in treeless areas, but keeps a constant "Whoosh!" going outside the tent.

By now, the seriousness of my situation had begun setting in. Already, moisture was forming inside the sleeping bag. It would freeze when I would partially emerge to shove the gathering snow from the front flap. The ice would then melt when I sealed it up again, soaking my clothes. When I emerged the next time, I would find ice next to my skin. Time after time this went on until I was virtually encased in a thin sheet of ice. The only cure for this was to get the clothes dried out by a fire, but my hopes of that disappeared with the last few strawberry drops of Sterno.

The chilling of my body went on. The first two fingers of my left hand hadn't completely thawed since the dog died, and were stiff and useless like sticks of wood. My bad ear from the first trip was alternately freezing and thawing, creating an intense burning pain. In a way, that was good, because the pain helped me stay awake—and I dared not fall asleep.

The old wives' tale about falling asleep and freezing to death worked well in Jack London's excellent story "To Build A Fire," but the truth is, if a man is in that cold a situation, without heat from an outside source, he'll freeze to death whether he's awake or asleep. In my circumstances, however, I was in danger of being smothered by blowing snow, and only my hourly diligent few minutes of scooping and pounding kept me uncovered. The task became increasingly difficult as the night wore on. Several inches of the finely-sifted powder lay on every piece of gear I had, and I could no longer open the front flap to shove it out. My fingers had lost their capacity for fine manipulation.

When the first waves of dizziness came over me, close to morning, I knew I was in deep trouble. When hypothermia causes the body temperature to drop, the mind plays tricks on a man.

I told myself, "Whatever happens, you will not leave this tent! Nothing can live outside this tent! Stay inside!"

As a person about to go on a bender would tell himself, "No matter how drunk you get, you will *not* drive home!" the message stayed with me.

Of the hours of delirium that followed, I remember very few things. At the outset, I was determined to keep my mind working. I found my journal in a parka pocket and wrote several shaky sentences before the hand ceased to function. With my left hand, I pulled the pen out of the right, and then beat the hand flat until it slipped back into the big mitten. Writing was obviously out of the question.

What I needed to do was read, but I couldn't turn the pages of the little book I had brought. Fishing around under the dusty snowpile again, I came upon a can of Spam in the foodstuffs. Eating it was not in the cards, as it had frozen to a brick, but the can had writing on it, and I intended to read it.

Whenever I felt the silliness of what the Indians call the "cold drunk" (*deskáss codáy*) come over me, I would read the can of Spam. This project seemed to help some, but more and more quickly, the words would fade, and I found myself thinking, "What do I care if Spam is the registered trademark of a pork product processed by the Geo. A. Hormel Company in Austin, Minnesota?"

To keep my mind off the cold of my body, I thought of other things. I recall wondering what the Spam plant in Austin, Minnesota looked like. Then I would remember that Minnesota gets cold in the winter, and I would get cold again.

The cold that comes in an Arctic storm is not, as scientists would have you believe, merely the absence of heat. The cold of the North is a terrible

200

sledge that slams the senses, renders strong men useless, and weak men dead. It drives the nearly indestructible moose into hiding. The cold is everywhere, like smoke, and seeps in openings in clothing and bedding you weren't aware you had. Everywhere it finds flesh, it numbs like novacaine. It is a total condition. It strikes everything, and only the brave flames of a fire can protect a man.

But I had no fire.

The jelling of the Coleman fuel for the stove was a real sore point with me. For the best part of an hour, during lucid moments, I mapped out the nasty letter I was going to send to the company. When polished, it was short and to the point:

A tent
Eight miles from Sagwon
Alaska

Dear Mr. Coleman:

This is to inform you that the fuel you sell for your little Coleman one-burner camp stove doesn't work at less than forty degrees below zero fahrenheit.

I hope you realize that I may very well freeze to death because of the failure of your fuel to burn. In the future, please refrain from showing nothing but happy campers in the pamphlets you distribute. Show a picture of someone

201

in a stupid Army tent in the foothills of the stupid Brooks Range freezing to stupid death because he couldn't do anything with the stupid fuel but spread it on a piece of stupid bread.

In short, Mr. Coleman, and before I enter my terminal stages of hypothermia, I would just like to say (and please excuse the pun) that I wish your fuel was made of Sterno stuff!

With warm regards but a cold stove,
Slim Randles

With the letter totally put together in my mind, I began to wonder what effect the letter would have on the future of cold-weather camping. Would Mr. Coleman immediately call in his top engineers and say, "Well boys, here's Slim's letter, now let's get on with it, and come up with a stove fuel that can be used all year round in beautiful Eight-Miles-From-Sagwon."

Actually, I felt that my chances were better of receiving the following reply.

Dear Mr. Randles:
In regard to your letter of Nov. 21, 1970, thanks for your interest in Coleman camping products.

Also, why don't you do your camping in the summer like sane people do?

Sincerely,
Mr. Coleman

The thought of receiving that letter from Mr. Coleman discouraged me from ever writing the first one, so I guess we'll never know.

But my preoccupation with the correspondence between the Coleman people and myself was short-lived. Before much longer, my eyes wouldn't focus properly—the tiny muscles needed for the operation had ceased to function. The panic of a person suddenly blinded came on me. I even began to miss reading the can of Spam. In fact, that can of Spam became very important to me. I shielded it against the cold inside of my sleeping bag with my other valuables, as though it were a talisman of proper sight.

In my half-lucid frame of mind, I felt the aircraft beacon and considered turning it on. After all, I thought, this was an emergency, and I could remember that I was only to use it in case of emergency. Then, trying hard, I was able to reason that the pipeline men *knew* I was in trouble, and they also knew my approximate location, and they couldn't fly in this storm anyway.

I was totally cut off. They couldn't come at all.

After that, I remember little except vague dreams that would come across my mind as I drifted in and out of consciousness.

Always, though, I remembered to stay inside the tent. "Nothing can live outside the tent!"

With the illogical logic known to us in dreams, I then reasoned that the dogs had all died. They were outside the tent. Nothing outside the tent could live. Therefore the dogs were now dead. I turned on the walkie-talkie once and heard nothing. The men at the camps were dead. The camps were outside the tent. If they were dead, then *everything* outside the tent was dead.

What would I do? This problem kept flashing through what was left of my thinking processes. I began to drag in wisps of thought and swirl them together into a misty plan. If the storm let up before I died, I would walk south until I found a warm climate, and build a house and find something to eat if I could. But I would have to get warm . . . that was first . . . I would have to get warm.

All my friends and family had died in the storm . . . I *knew* that by now. They weren't in the tent. If only the tent were bigger, I could get some people in it with me, and we could all live . . .

I barely heard the chopper's engine approaching, some thirty-two hours after I had last seen it. The men's hands were gentle and firm as they dug down and pulled me out of the tent. I recall asking them, when we were in the heated helicopter and they gave me sips of coffee, how they managed to stay alive in the storm. Did they have tents? They were kind, and said I'd be in a warm camp pretty soon.

Later, I was to learn that Big Mike had somehow wrapped the picket line around a front leg, cutting off circulation. The leg was amputated in Fairbanks.

The pilot had flown even before it was totally safe to do so. The temperature was minus eighteen, with a twenty-five-knot wind blowing when they found me, putting the chill factor at seventy-five degrees below zero.

The men had found me by spotting two inches of tent that still showed above the snow, and the red-painted driving bow of the big freight sled. Some men later flew out and took the whole team and the equipment to Sagwon, and several days later, to Fairbanks.

Even before "Doc" Jose Harrison called a halt to the trip, I knew it was over. George dead. Mike's leg gone. Two of my fingers in pretty bad shape. It was over.

A springtime trip might have gotten through. More daylight, crusted snow, fewer storms. It can be done. But not by me—not in this life.

30

Two days later, I looked back to see the airstrip at Sagwon disappear slowly beneath the wing of the plane. We climbed and headed south through the chilled peaks of the Brooks Range.

Doc Harrison, in an attempt to make me feel better, pointed out Dietrich Pass, lying frozen and windswept beneath us.

"You'd have never made it over that pass, Son. It was just too much to try for."

Maybe it was. Maybe it's impossible—but I doubt it.

Mother Nature occasionally lets a man slip through. She hadn't this time, but it happens. It took Peary many tries, over more than twenty years, to reach the North Pole. It took nearly more than he had to give to make it, but he made it. And yet, one storm such as the one that had just swept the

Slope, and Peary's final expedition would have failed.

The ways of the North are strange. It seems at times to operate on whims and fancies. Sometimes, the North appears to take pride in or pity on a lone straggler, and magically, the traveler finds good weather, packed trails, and fresh dogs to the end of the trail. Conversely, sometimes the best-equipped expeditions get through, and at other times are stopped cold, with the entire group perishing.

Sir John Franklin, the man for whom the Franklin Bluffs were named, took two fully-equipped ships and one-hundred twenty-nine men into the North in the late 1840's. No one ever knows for certain how the men died, but they all perished.

And then there was Hubert Darrell.

Darrell, whom even the Eskimos thought crazy, walked alone, without dogs, thousands of miles through the Arctic pulling a hand sled in the early years of this century. How he made it through alone when well-equipped parties perished, is again one of the whims of the North. In 1910, Darrell set out on another thousand-mile trip, and was never heard from again.

But the North itself is to blame for all these tries. Not only does it sometimes kill with abandon, but it also surprises, delights, and uplifts the fortunate man who takes the country as his own.

207

Since the first people crossed the ice to this land, it has alternately killed them in storms, at sea, and on trail; and has treated them to sights that few of the earth's populations have witnessed.

The country is in itself a magic, a burning, a restless challenge. Few people who live with the bush on its own terms can resist the drive to see more, to feel more, to explore the places most men only dream about.

The country defeats much more often than it is conquered. But, as if in consolation, it also gives a liberal dose of a feeling of conquest along with the defeat. For each slam, there is hope and drive to continue. It has been that way since man first stood and looked at the pearly moonlit peaks of the Alaska Range, or saw the swirling Northern Lights playing across the stage.

And so it will continue until some space age developer decides to level the mountains and build housing tracts on them. Only then will the gloss and verve leave this land.

When that day comes, the developer will also meet great defeats as the country struggles in its death throes. Each time a person puts on snowshoes and crunches through an uncharted valley, the bush gives up a little bit of its mystery, but not without first exacting her price.

This book has been the story of two defeats at the

208

hands of Nature—the first by a lack of snow; the second through a ground blizzard. But though the objectives weren't reached, the trips gave more in personal satisfaction and just plain living, than they took away in defeat.

And still, as I write, the visions of packed trails, moonglow on the snowfields, and the eager lunge of a team, are irrepressible.

As the sourdoughs always say cheerfully, "Next year will be better, just wait and see!"

And the sourdoughs are always right.

Slim Randles
Talkeetna, Alaska
January, 1972